I0796880

The Spell Dispensary

·•☽☽○☾☾•·

200 spells and rituals for healing magick and manifestation

Deb Robinson

VERBENA

Contents

I dedicate this book to my daughter, Ella,
without whom none of this would be possible.

I love you, Ella.

"When I feel disconnected,
you're all that I need."

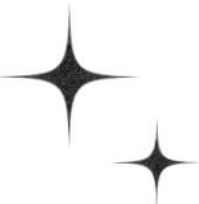

Merry Meet

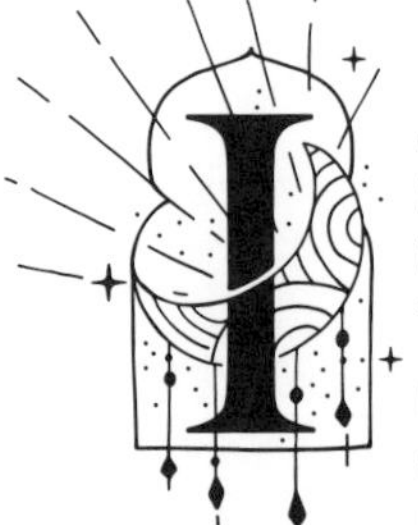

I am Deb – a practicing witch raised, and living, in Yorkshire, England. I have always believed in magick, as I guess most children do, but the thing is, I didn't ever stop believing!

Magick was always encouraged throughout my early life and that of my three siblings. Though my parents weren't well-off, they would enrich our childhood by encouraging a world of make-believe where anything was possible: an ordinary rug became a flying carpet that would carry my twin sister and me to all the places of our imagination (though of course, it only worked when we shut our eyes!); sticks were magick wands; daisies were for divination; and dandelion clocks were for wishes.

I didn't want to leave that magick behind. I knew in my soul that magick was real, and though as I grew I fast realised that the rug didn't fly, I still believed in the power of intention and visualisation, and I realised early on that I had the power to manifest my desires.

The first time I realised I had some kind of ability – a 'knowing' if you like – was when I was a teenager. I was sitting on the back seat of the bus when I saw someone walking across the bus station; someone I had never seen before in my life. "That's the person I'm going to marry", I stated to the friend I was with. And sure enough, a few years later, we did marry, and almost forty years later we are still together.

I have always studied witchcraft and divination, though I didn't always identify as a witch – this came later, after hearing the rumours that my maternal great, great grandmother was a 'fortune teller' who would travel from place-to-place reading tarot. After hearing this I was inspired to

delve deeper into tarot reading myself. It was then that I discovered my own natural ability to read intuitively, and from that moment I really started to focus on my own witchcraft journey, and to truly identify as a witch.

As my passion for the craft grew, so did a desire to make witchcraft more accessible, to empower other people to embrace magick and manifest the life they desired. It frustrated me that witchcraft was stigmatised and misunderstood, and I set out on a mission to change this.

So, with my daughter Ella, I opened our beautiful family-owned magick emporium, Practical Magick, in the heart of Yorkshire, England. It was a busy little magick shop filled with love, warmth, and positive energy. The shop gained an amazing reputation and people from all spiritual paths would come to visit us, often from overseas, to purchase our wares and have me read their tarot cards – such was Practical Magick's popularity! During this time, I would also offer a house-cleansing service (which our customers fondly referred to as my 'ghostbusting'), where I would go to people's houses and perform cleaning rituals to raise the vibration of their home and clear any stagnant or negative energies.

Then, with a mission to deliver our magick worldwide, in November 2016 Ella and I launched our magickal monthly subscription box, Witch Casket, and we could not have known then that it would become so popular so quickly! It wasn't long before Witch Casket became a full-time passion, and we have dedicated our lives to it ever since.

To this day, with Witch Casket, we continue to share our magick, not only here in Yorkshire, but all across this glorious

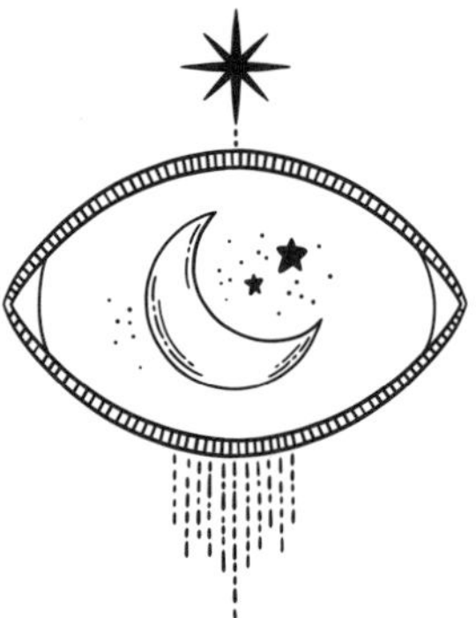

planet! It is so heart-warming to know that witches worldwide are learning from my lifetime of study and knowledge; performing my tried and trusted spells and rituals; working with the divination tools that I have created; and being empowered to live their authentic, magickal lives!

Last year I wrote, *The Witch-ionary: An A-Z of magickal terms and their meanings,* and it was hugely rewarding to see my little dictionary of witchcraft gracing the bookshelves of witches everywhere! With that, I had manifested one of my dreams... but my ultimate dream is to teach others to manifest their desires too.

With this in mind, I have written *The Spell Dispensary,* a book of over 200 magick spells and rituals curated to help people with everyday issues, to empower people to practice magick and put their faith in the power of their own intent and belief. If we intend something, and we truly believe in it, and we work hard towards it, it will be ours. But if we don't set that intention, or have that belief, no amount of hard work can bring us our desired outcome. Once you know your power, nothing can stop you!

Everything in the Universe has its own unique vibration, and working with the energies of crystals, herbs, flowers, and so on, can raise our own vibration – which in turn attracts. If we have a vibration of joy, we will attract more joy, for example, and once you realise how important the energy you put out into the world is, you'll do everything you can to work with it.

My aim when writing *The Spell Dispensary* was simple: I wanted to create a spell book for ordinary people. So many spell books have endless lists of 'ingredients' that are so obscure they're almost impossible to find. I focused on curating spells that use only things that are easy-to-find and inexpensive. There is little

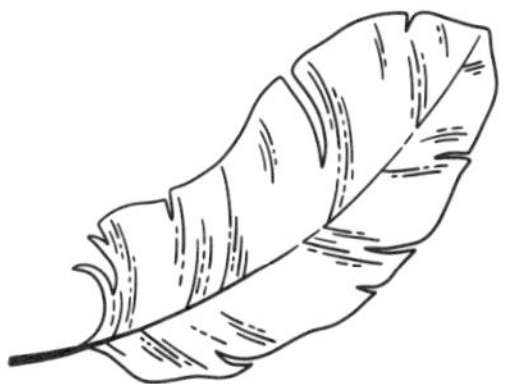

point in a spell book if you can't easily source the items you need. Additionally, you won't find any spells in this book that aren't completely cruelty-free: you won't have a need for bones, or blood, for example. Furthermore, you won't find a need for your own blood, or hair, or nail-clippings. I have deliberately curated a book that can comfortably be used by witches and aspiring witches of all ages regardless of how new they are to witchcraft. But that's not to say that experienced witches won't find what they need too – this book is inclusive, and is for anyone who wants to practice witchcraft safely. Just because the spells are easy-to-follow doesn't mean they aren't powerful; these are tried and trusted spells from my own personal Book of Shadows, and I am honoured to be able to share them with you.

It is important for you to know that if a spell calls for you to stand, and you are unable to do so, by all means, sit; and if it calls for you to state something out loud, and you are unable to do so, thinking the words holds just as much power. If there's an item you don't have, you can substitute it for another item with the same properties, and if a particular incantation feels 'off' to you, use your own words. Spell craft is a great passion of mine, and I love encouraging people to have input in the spells they are casting, so please, please, feel free to make my spells your own. The beauty and magick of witchcraft is that it follows no set path, and has no hard, fast rules; rather, it is a labyrinth through which we each find our own path, learning, and growing as we go. Just like my first book, *The Witch-ionary*, I hope you find this book is another useful guide for you on your witchcraft journey.

How this Book Works

The categories in *The Spell Dispensary* are arranged alphabetically to make it easy for you to find a spell for a particular purpose. The spells within each category are not alphabetical, and I would urge you to read through them and use the one which resonates most, and for which you have the required items (or suitable substitutes).

A Few Notes on Ingredients and Tools

Herbs, Flowers, and Spices

When working with herbs, flowers, spices, and so on, where a spell does not state the quantity required, that is because it's not critical to the outcome of the spell. Let your intuition guide the quantities you use. The intention that you put into your practice is more important – so use a good measure of that!

Where the nature of a herb or spice is not stated in the ingredients list – whether they are dried, ground, or fresh – it is a general rule of thumb that for spells such as charm bags and spells jars (where the plants will be 'stored' for a while), dried is preferred so as to minimise the chance of mould. Where mould isn't a concern, either fresh, ground, or dried work equally well, so feel free to use whatever you have at hand.

Disposing of Organic Ingredients

Once you feel a spell no longer serves, organic ingredients should be returned to the earth with gratitude, and other items such as stones, crystals, bottles, or bags, can be cleansed for reuse.

Oils

Pure essential oils must never be ingested and should always be diluted before applying to the skin. Also, be mindful of allergies (please see important safety information provided). The culinary oils mentioned in this book are safe to consume and can also be used as carrier oils to dilute the essential oils.

Moon Water

Some spells in this book require 'moon water'. Briefly, moon water is any water that has been set out in the moonlight to absorb the lunar energy. If the moon water you make is for a spell where the water will be ingested, always use fresh drinking water to make it, and consume within 24 hours. If you will not be ingesting the moon water, simply using it in other spell craft, any water can be used, and this can be stored for up to a couple of weeks.

Crystals

It is always good practise to cleanse your crystals before use. This will dispel any residual negative energy and ready them for use. Here are a few simple methods you can use:

- Leave the crystals to bask in the moonlight to absorb the magickal lunar energy.
- Allow running water to flow over them. Visualise all negative energy being rinsed away by this pure, natural element. Be mindful that soft stones such as selenite, celestite, and angelite, should not be cleansed in this way.
- Half fill a jar with salt. Ensure your crystals are dry before placing them in the jar, then leave them overnight. The salt will absorb any negative energy from the crystal, so it should be discarded after use.
- Burying crystals in the earth is a perfect method of cleansing them, since crystals originate from the earth. Soft crystals should not be left for long if the earth is moist as they may begin to dissolve.
- Selenite is a perfect solution for cleaning crystals, in particular soft, fragile crystals that may suffer from the previously suggested methods. Lay crystals on or very close to selenite and let them sit there for several hours.

Altar Tools

No tool is essential to a witch. A pan works as well as a cauldron, a finger works as well as a wand, and a notebook or even a Word document can take the place of a Book of Shadows. Don't ever feel pressured to 'have' things. If you want them, they can help you to direct your energy or focus your magick – but the most important things are your intent and belief, and if you have these in abundance, you will be as powerful as any witch.

Candles

Where a spell calls for a candle, it is practical to use a small spell candle, unless a tealight or floating candle is specified.

Some Magickal Terms Used in this Book

Intention

Charging the items you will use in your spells and infusing them with your own energy and intent is very important. To charge an item, free your mind from any negativity, then take the item in the palm of your hand. Feel a connection to it and imagine a white light emanating from it and surrounding you completely. Once you feel fully connected to your chosen item, meditate on your intention and see what you desire as if it were already realised. Continue until you feel your intention is set.

Grounding and Centering

To ground yourself, stand with the soles of your feet firmly on the ground. Visualise 'roots' sprouting from the soles of your feet and reaching deep into the earth below. Imagine these 'roots' reaching down into the earth, through any carpets, floorboards, or space that separate you from the earth. Visualise the grounding energy from the earth like a white light, flooding through your entire body, cleansing and renewing, from the soles of your feet right to the top of your head – then outwards, surrounding you in a beautiful, grounding light. Once you feel grounded, cleansed, and renewed, slowly draw up your 'roots', and feel gratitude to Mother Earth.

Centre yourself by focusing on any scattered energy that you feel within and around you. Visualise those energies rolling together like liquid metal or water droplets, coming together in a pool, which turns into a ball of powerful, focused energy that you have control over. You can then align this energy with your intention and use it during your magickal workings. Once your spell work is completed, you can rid yourself of this intense energy by grounding yourself and releasing it into the earth.

Spirit

In this book when I mention Spirit, I am referring to the unseen connection between the witch and 'the other' – Spirit is what you connect to (often during divination) when seeking insight or wisdom. Spirit is a mystery and will depend on your own personal beliefs; some would say they are connecting to a deity; others believe they are connecting to spirit guides, or angels, or the 'Universe'.

Ethics

It is my strong belief that a witch's ethics are their own business. But all the same, magick should be practiced with care. Some witches believe in the 'rule of three', meaning that anything you put out into the Universe will come back to you threefold. The Wiccan Rede, for those who identify as Wiccan, states in its closing line "An ye harm none, do what ye will", suggesting that followers of Wicca are free to practice in any way they choose, so long as they cause no harm.

Important Safety Information

Allergies

Please be mindful of allergies – where a spell requires you to apply something to your skin, or add it to your bath, or consume it, substitute the item for another with similar magickal properties if you have an allergy.

Fire Safety

Where a spell calls for candles, incense, or fire in any form, work with fire safety in mind, be cautious of anything nearby that could be flammable, and don't ever leave burning materials unattended.

ABUNDANCE

Candle Spell for Abundance

A simple, yet beautiful candle spell to attract abundance.

YOU WILL NEED:

- Cinnamon
- Mint
- Almond oil
- Green spell candle

Grind the cinnamon and mint together, clockwise, with the intention to attract abundance – think about exactly what you would like to welcome into your life.

Add your blend to the almond oil and use your magickal oil to anoint your spell candle. Dress the candle towards you to attract.

Light the candle, and as it burns sit quietly and visualise your successful outcome.

Abundance Boundary Wash

Attract abundance into your home by creating a magickal boundary wash.

YOU WILL NEED:

- Peppermint essential oil
- Bergamot essential oil

Add a few drops of each oil to warm water, stir the water clockwise with the intention to attract abundance to your home.

Use this water to wash your door and window frames. This will raise the vibration in your home and attract abundance and good fortune.

Abundance Witches' Brew

Raise your vibration to attract abundance with this delicious magickal brew.

YOU WILL NEED:

* Red clover
* Chamomile
* Tea infuser

Add your herbs to your infuser and place in a cup of hot (previously boiled) water.

Allow to steep for three to five minutes.

Remove the infuser.

Stir your brew clockwise, stating the following:

"I will attract whatever I need,

With this brew I plant the seed,

As I drink my energy attracts

An abundance of all that I lack."

Drink mindfully, and with gratitude.

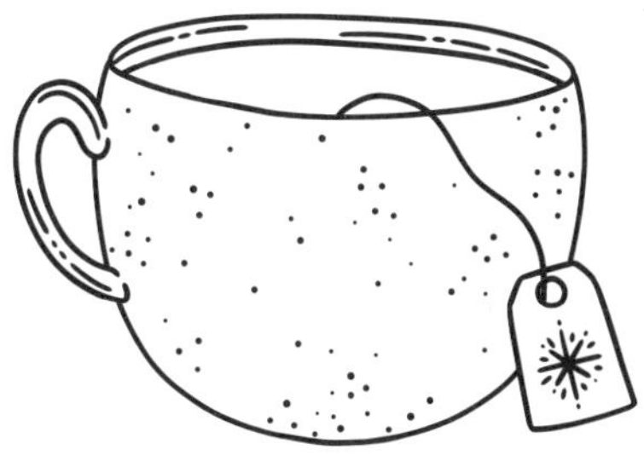

Potion to Attract Abundance

An all-purpose potion to use in spells and rituals for abundance.

YOU WILL NEED:

* Chamomile
* Orange peel
* Moss agate crystal

Add the chamomile, orange peel, and moss agate to a pan of warm water. As you stir clockwise, set your intention and chant the following:

"Fragrant fruit, stone, and flower,

Nature's treasures infuse thy power,

Abundance is what I decree,

As I will it, so mote it be."

Allow the infusion to cool, then remove the crystal and bottle the infusion. The crystal can be carried with you in your wallet or pocket to attract abundance.

The infusion can be used to anoint candles, add to ritual baths, or as a magickal room or aura spray etc. Any infusion that will not be used within two days can be frozen in ice cube trays to preserve it in useable amounts.

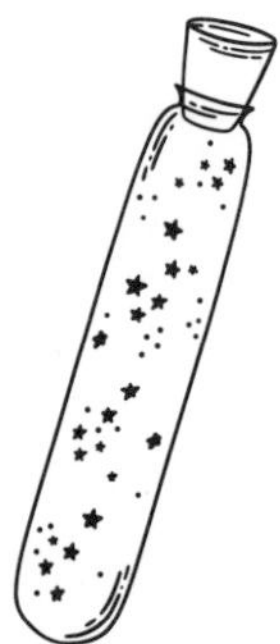

Abundance Braid

A mindful spell to create a beautiful braid to keep at the entrance to your home.

YOU WILL NEED:

- Green or white spell candle
- Small bundle of long grass

At a time of peace, when you can work uninterrupted, light your candle and, as it burns, peacefully braid the grass. It doesn't matter if you are good at this or not, so long as you work with intent.

As you braid, state the following:

"May the blessing of nature's harvest bring abundance to my home.

I thank the Universe for the gifts I have, and those yet to come.

As I braid this grass, I cast a spell filled with love and positivity

That only brightest blessings will come to me."

Once finished, place your braid at the entrance to your home to welcome abundance and blessings.

Charm Bag for Abundance

An enchanting pouch to keep with you to attract what you desire, in abundance.

YOU WILL NEED:

* Lemongrass
* Cloves
* Green aventurine or citrine crystal
* Green or white drawstring pouch

Blend your lemongrass and cloves clockwise, while you focus your intent: that these magickal herbs will bring abundance your way. This could be any kind of abundance: financial abundance, an abundance of love, or joy, or healing etc.

Repeat the following as you blend your herbs – and do so with gratitude that what you need is coming your way.

"Hear clearly the words I speak,

Bring to me the abundance I seek,

With joy, I attract all that I need,

With gratitude I receive it at speed."

Sit with the crystal and charge it with your intentions before adding this to the pouch.

Add your herb blend to the pouch; and feel free to add in anything else that you feel symbolises the type of abundance you seek.

Keep your charm bag close knowing abundance is on its way!

Recharge as necessary until you feel this no longer serves, at which point you can give the herbs back to the earth with thanks and cleanse the pouch and crystal for reuse.

Abundance Fire Bowl

A powerful fire spell for abundance!

YOU WILL NEED:

* Fire-proof bowl
* Rock salt
* Cinnamon
* Dried apple slices
* Pen and paper
* Length of string

Place your fire-proof bowl on a heat-proof surface.

Place your salt in the bowl, working clockwise to attract, then sprinkle the cinnamon, and add the apple slices.

Take your paper and note down the abundance you need. This can be an abundance of love, money, creativity etc. Fold the paper, always folding towards you, as many times as possible and tie it firmly with the string.

Place the paper bundle in the bowl on top of your salt, cinnamon and apple, and light it. As it burns visualise your desires being met, and the abundance you seek.

Keep the abundance bowl in your magickal space until you feel it no longer serves.

ALL-PURPOSE MANIFESTATION

Versatile Knot Magick Spell

Whatever you need, this simple knot magick spell will help you to attract it.

YOU WILL NEED:

* Length of string
* Key
* Cinnamon stick
* Root ginger
* Safety pin

Tie four knots into the string – tying one of the above items into each knot.

Think about what you desire – as you tie each knot, chant the following while imagining your desired outcome:

Knot one: ***"Cinnamon to attract what I need."***

Knot two: ***"Ginger to make it come at speed."***

Knot three: ***"A key to lock my intentions in."***

Knot four: ***"Adding safety, with this pin."***

Hang this knotted charm in your home to attract what you desire.

Enchanting All-Purpose Charm Bag

Carry with you the power to attract what you desire with this beautiful charm bag spell.

YOU WILL NEED:

* Green or white drawstring pouch
* Mint
* Patchouli leaf
* Juniper berries
* Citrine crystal

Think about what it is that you need in your life. Sit with each item and set your intention, imagining a positive outcome.

Add each item to your pouch mindfully.

Tie your pouch firmly closed.

Keep your charm bag with you until you feel it no longer serves.

Steamy Manifestation

An uncomplicated way to set intentions and see your goals manifested.

Take a hot bath or shower and visualise what you would like to attract to you – love, money, health etc.

Afterwards, look into your steamed-up bathroom mirror, and write or draw sigils relating to what you desire.

Notice your image in the mirror blended with your wishes, representing that you and your desires will come together, and give gratitude for what is about to come.

Manifestation Bowl

A bowl to attract what you desire.

YOU WILL NEED:

- Rice
- Almonds
- Dried orange peel
- Basil
- Mint

Place all the ingredients into the bowl. Now add in something that represents what it is you'd like to manifest and say:

"Universe, I ask of thee,

Bring my desire right to me,

As I will it, so mote it be."

You can 'feed' your bowl by adding items that represent what it is you'd like to manifest, each time resetting your intention. Once you feel your bowl is fully charged, leave it until your goal is met.

Planting Spell

Planting things that represent your desires, with the intention that they grow into reality, can be very powerful. Only bury things that will not harm the earth, such as herbs, leaves, stones, untreated paper etc. If it came from the earth, we can give it to the earth.

Choose something to represent your desire. Your planting ritual can be as simple as writing that on a leaf and burying it with the intention that it will come to pass. As you plant, say:

"Fertile earth I plant in thee,

With intent that my dreams will be,

Grow my wishes – make them come true,

I give gratitude and love to you."

Wish Come True Candle Spell

A gentle spell to help your wishes come true.

YOU WILL NEED:

- Something sharp, like a pin or darning needle
- Small white candle
- Lodestone oil
- Cloves
- Star anise

Take your sharp object and etch into your candle any sigils, words, or images that represent your wish.

Anoint the candle working towards you with lodestone oil, stating the outcome you wish to attract.

Place your candle in a suitable holder, and circle it with star anise and cloves, working clockwise.

Light your candle. As it burns, visualise your wish being realised and feel the emotions and gratitude as you know your wish will soon come true.

Candle Manifestation

A simple yet powerful ritual to help you achieve your desires.

YOU WILL NEED:

* Rosemary
* Dandelion leaf
* Orange spell candle

Blend the rosemary and dandelion leaf together whilst setting your intentions.

Circle the candle with your herb blend, working clockwise.

Light the candle and state the following:

"I send my wish in this flickering fire,

I attract what I desire,

What I wish is coming to me,

As I will it, so mote it be."

Meditate as the candle burns down, and visualise your desires being met.

ALTAR PROTECTION & BLESSING

Altar Blessing Charm Bag

A magickal pouch to protect your sacred space and encourage insight and wisdom.

YOU WILL NEED:

- Chamomile
- Bay leaves
- Amethyst chips
- White drawstring pouch

Add the chamomile to the protection pouch and state the following:

"Chamomile to promote peace and harmony"

Add the bay leaves to the protection pouch and state the following:

"Protective power, I draw on thee"

Add the amethyst chips to the protection pouch and state the following:

"Amethyst to help me see"

Pull the pouch closed and state:

"Peace, protection, and insight I draw to me,

As I will it, so mote it be."

Keep the pouch in your magickal space to offer peace, protection, and insight.

Candle Ritual for Altar Blessing

A beautiful ritual to cleanse and bless your altar or sacred space and ensure you have a tranquil place to work your magick.

YOU WILL NEED:

* White spell candle
* Mint
* Dill weed
* Cloves
* Quartz crystal chips

Place your spell candle in a suitable holder.

Encircle it with the mint, dill weed, and quartz crystal chips – create your circle of herbs and crystals clockwise in order to attract blessings.

Light the candle and state the following:

"Negativity, leave this place,

Good vibrations, take its place,

Blessings I attract to me,

As I will it, so mote it be."

As the candle burns, your sacred space will be cleansed and blessed – leaving you with good energy to work your craft.

Bless your Altar Tools

It is recommended to regularly cleanse your altar tools so they don't carry with them any stagnant energies from past spells or rituals.

YOU WILL NEED:

* Incense (sandalwood, dragon's blood, frankincense and lavender are good choices)

Light your incense.

Take each tool you will be using and pass it through the incense smoke to bless it, stating the following:

"Negative energy, in this smoke be drowned,

All that's bad be turned around,

With good intentions, and no one harmed,

My magickal tools are blessed and charmed."

Altar Blessing Bowl

A beautiful, magickal bowl to absorb any negativity from your altar.

YOU WILL NEED:

* Bowl
* Uncooked rice
* Dried lemon peel
* Red clover
* Marigold

Half-fill your bowl with a base of rice. Mindfully add in the other items, with intent that your magickal bowl will bless and protect. Keep this bowl in your magickal space to absorb any negativity. Once you feel its work is done, take the contents far from home and return them to the earth with thanks.

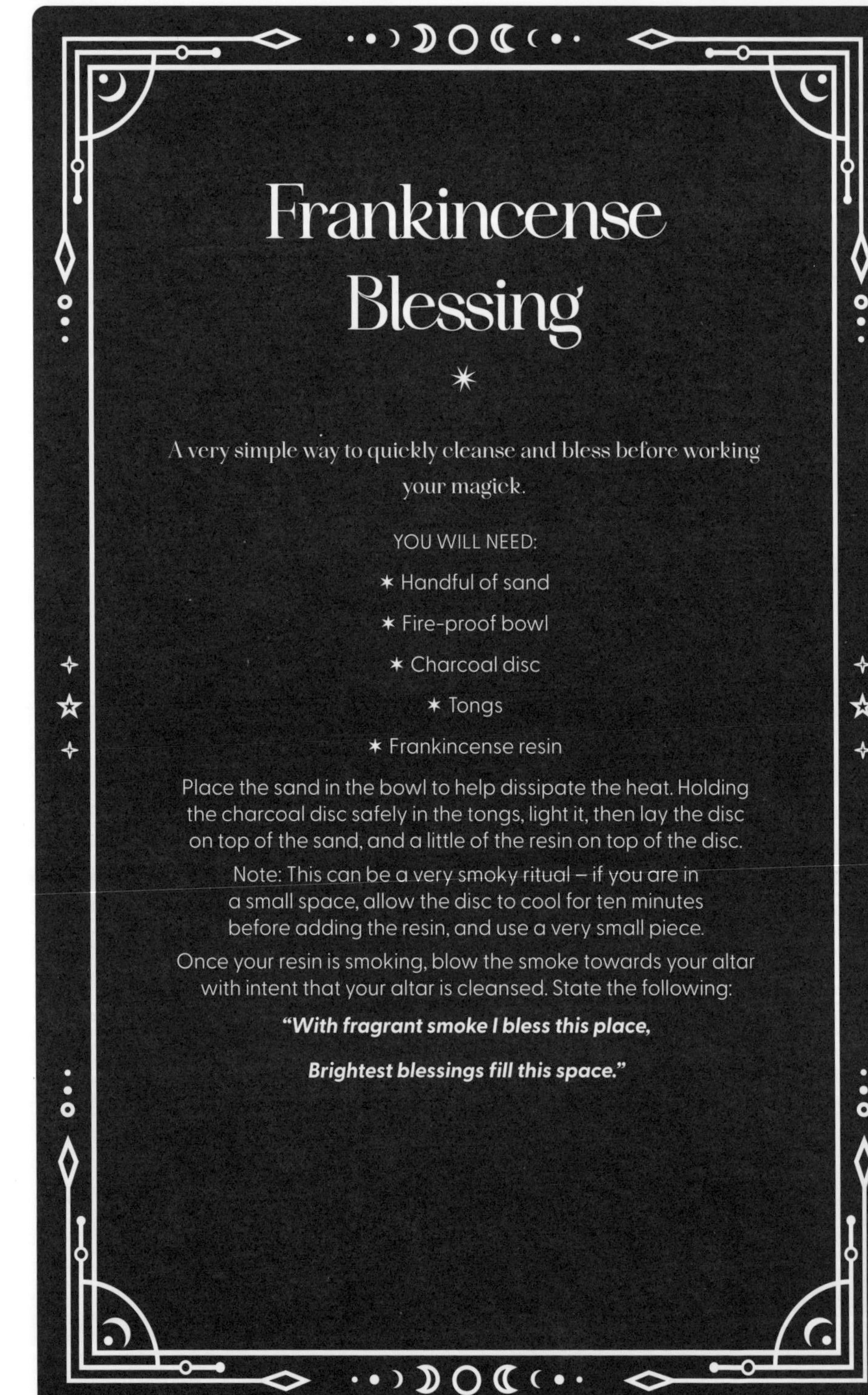

Frankincense Blessing

A very simple way to quickly cleanse and bless before working your magick.

YOU WILL NEED:

* Handful of sand
* Fire-proof bowl
* Charcoal disc
* Tongs
* Frankincense resin

Place the sand in the bowl to help dissipate the heat. Holding the charcoal disc safely in the tongs, light it, then lay the disc on top of the sand, and a little of the resin on top of the disc.

Note: This can be a very smoky ritual – if you are in a small space, allow the disc to cool for ten minutes before adding the resin, and use a very small piece.

Once your resin is smoking, blow the smoke towards your altar with intent that your altar is cleansed. State the following:

"With fragrant smoke I bless this place,

Brightest blessings fill this space."

Cleansing Aura Spray

Use this spray to cleanse the aura around yourself and your altar before working your magick.

YOU WILL NEED:

* Citronella, bergamot, and lavender essential oils
* 1 cup (250ml) moon water
* Spray bottle

Add a few drops of each of the three essential oils to a cup of moon water. Pour the magickal liquid into a spray bottle or atomiser and use this to spray your altar space, and your aura to cleanse and bless.

If you need to preserve your spray for future use, use water mixed with alcohol (the alcohol should have a minimum of 60% ethanol content).

Altar Blessing with Wand or Athame

Once you have your altar set up as you wish, you can use a wand or athame to bless it and your altar tools.

Ground and centre yourself. Use your wand or athame to direct your energy, and working clockwise point to each item on your altar as you state the following:

"Blessed be my magickal tools, may they serve me well as I work my magick.

May they work to serve my craft, with harm to none, and good for all."

Place your wand or athame on your altar and state:

"Blessed be this altar."

ANTI-ANXIETY & CALMING

Candle Spell to Banish Anxiety

A calming spell for anyone suffering from anxiety.

YOU WILL NEED:

* Something sharp, like a pin or darning needle
* Black or white spell candle
* Black peppercorns

Use the sharp object to etch into the candle something to represent what you feel anxious about.

Place the candle in a suitable candleholder. Circle the base of the candle with peppercorns, working counter-clockwise to banish your anxiety. Light the candle and state the following:

"I banish all anxiety,

As I will it, so mote it be."

Meditate as the candle burns, and feel your anxiety leaving with each breath you take.

Anxiety-Soothing Anointing Oil

Create a multi-purpose oil for use with all magickal workings to soothe anxiety.

YOU WILL NEED:

* 5 drops bergamot essential oil
* 5 drops ylang ylang essential oil
* 5 drops lavender essential oil
* 6 tsp olive oil

Blend the above oils together with intent. The anointing oil can then be used to anoint candles and magickal tools used for anti-anxiety spells. It can also be used to anoint your wrists and forehead, or as a calming bath oil.

Anti-Anxiety Fire Bowl

Send your stresses and anxieties up in smoke!

YOU WILL NEED:

- Pen and paper
- Dried nettle
- Dried thyme
- Fire-proof bowl

Note down the source or sources of your stress and anxiety. Blend the nettle and thyme counter-clockwise with the intention to banish anxiety. Fold up your note, and light it, then drop it into the bowl and watch it burn. As it burns chant:

"Smoke, carry my anxiety away,

And keep all my worries at bay."

Watch as your anxieties go up in smoke. Once the fire is burned out, carry the ashes far from home, bury them, and walk away without looking back.

Calming Charm Bag

Carry calming vibrations with you with this handy charm bag.

YOU WILL NEED:

- Amethyst
- Rose quartz
- Dried cedar leaf
- Valerian root
- Blue or white drawstring pouch

Sit with each item to set your intention, before adding it to the drawstring pouch. Tie the bag firmly closed. Sit quietly and connect with your pouch. Keep this nearby to keep anxiety at bay, and sit with it whenever you need to draw from its calming energy.

Anti-Anxiety Knot Magick

A mindful way to banish anxiety.

YOU WILL NEED:

- Long piece of string, ribbon, or cord

At a time when you feel calm and relaxed, sit with your string and set your intention – that the magickal knots you tie will represent your intention to keep anxiety at bay, and that as long at they remain tied, will keep your anxiety tied away too!

Then, firmly tie knots in the string and as you do so, state the following:

"Knot one, the spell's begun.

Knot two, it will be true.

Knot three, it shall be.

Knot four, it is lore.

Knot five, the magick's alive.

Knot six, the spell is fixed.

Knot seven, chance I'll leaven.

Knot eight, my will is fate.

Knot nine, it's sealed in twine."

You can also tie other objects, amulets, affirmations, or ribbons into your knots to represent your intent, though this is not essential – your intent is the most important thing to weave into your knots!

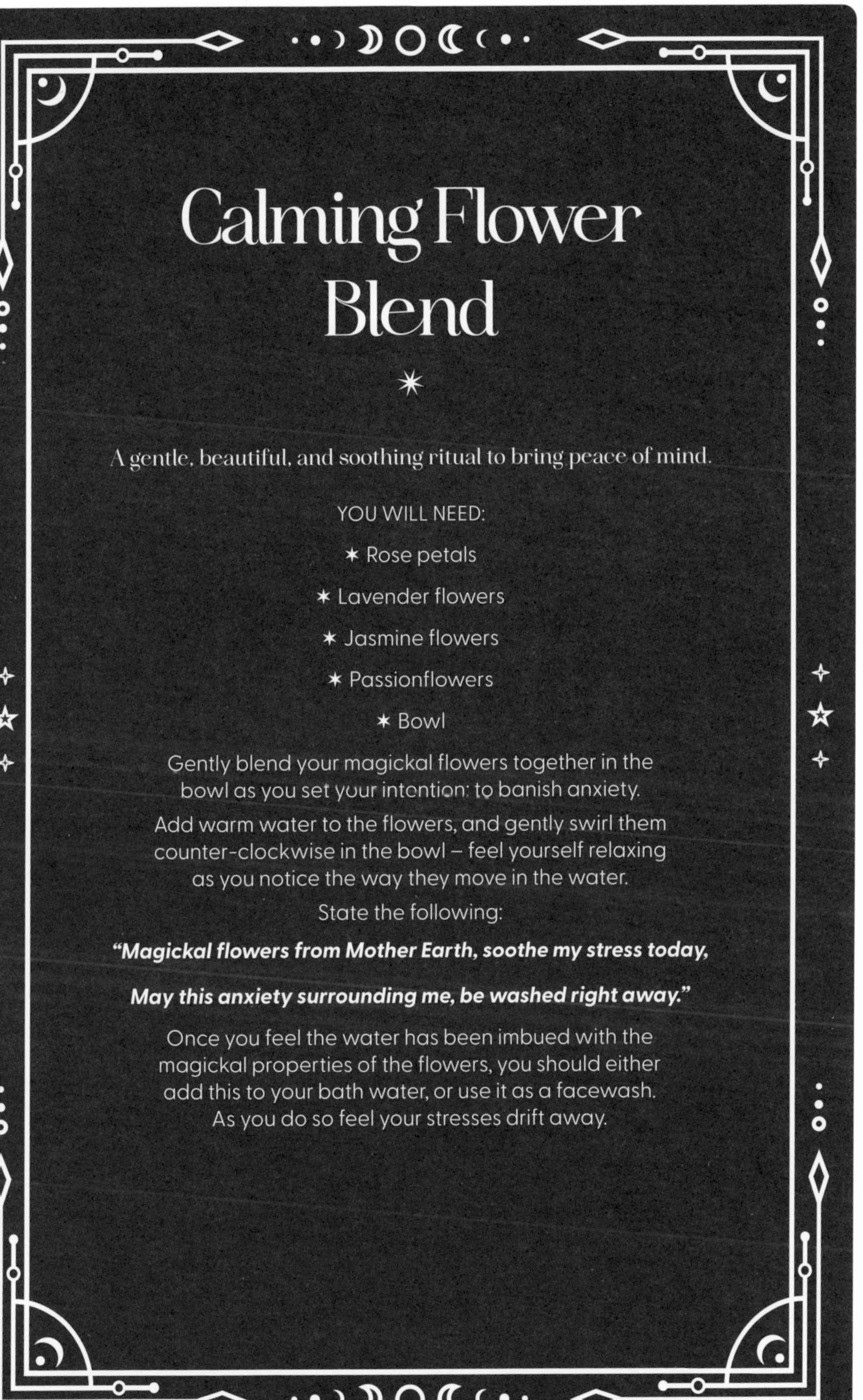

Calming Flower Blend

A gentle, beautiful, and soothing ritual to bring peace of mind.

YOU WILL NEED:

- Rose petals
- Lavender flowers
- Jasmine flowers
- Passionflowers
- Bowl

Gently blend your magickal flowers together in the bowl as you set your intention: to banish anxiety.

Add warm water to the flowers, and gently swirl them counter-clockwise in the bowl – feel yourself relaxing as you notice the way they move in the water.

State the following:

"Magickal flowers from Mother Earth, soothe my stress today,

May this anxiety surrounding me, be washed right away."

Once you feel the water has been imbued with the magickal properties of the flowers, you should either add this to your bath water, or use it as a facewash. As you do so feel your stresses drift away.

BANISHING

Negative Energy Removal Herb Bundle

Make a beautiful herb bundle to use to remove negative energy from your space.

YOU WILL NEED:

* Sprigs of dried rosemary
* Sprigs of dried eucalyptus
* Springs of dried lavender
* A length of string

Gather the plants together in a tight bundle. Secure with the string at one end, then wind the string tightly all the way down, stopping approximately 1–1½in (3–4cm) from the bottom. Wind back to the top, then back to the bottom, maintaining the tension in the string, and tie it off.

Holding your bundle over a plate or tray to catch any falling embers, light the bundle.

Walk around your room or home counter-clockwise, blowing the smoke gently into all corners, and state the following with intent:

"With this smoke, this space I clear,

Of energy that lingers here.

Negative energy, I banish thee,

As I will it, so mote it be."

Negativity Banishing Floor Wash

Cleanse your home and banish all negative vibrations with this simple floor wash.

YOU WILL NEED:

- Salt
- Rosemary
- Rue
- Vinegar

Add a little salt, rosemary, rue, and vinegar to a pan or cauldron of warm water. Stir counter-clockwise for banishing, and affirm:

"Negativity shall leave this place,

Only blessings enter my space.

Anything that would do me wrong,

It is my intention that it be gone!"

Strain the water and return the herbs to the earth with thanks. As you wash your floors (from the inside, towards the door) feel any negativity clearing and making way for only positive energies.

Banishing Candle Spell

If you have things in your life that you wish to rid yourself of, emotions or negative energies for example, here is a simple candle spell to help you to do just that.

YOU WILL NEED:

* Black spell candle
* Clove essential oil
* Ground black pepper

Anoint the black candle with clove oil, working away from you. Roll the candle in the black pepper, then light it, thinking about what you'd like to banish, and state the following with intent:

"With this fire, I banish thee,

As I will it, so mote it be."

Bury it Ritual

A magickal ritual to help you to bury your past.

YOU WILL NEED:

* Paper and pencil
* Cayenne pepper
* Marjoram
* Black spell candle
* Fire-proof dish

Note down the things you'd like to leave behind. Light the candle and visualise yourself moving on, empowered. Light the paper and allow it to burn in the fire-proof dish. Grind the ashes together counter-clockwise with the herbs, stating:

"No more power, I give to thee,

This magick spell will set me free."

Take the ash blend away from your home and bury it, to signify that you are burying your past. Walk away without looking back.

Banishing Spell Powder

Create a powder to banish that which no longer serves you.

YOU WILL NEED:

* Black pepper
* Rue
* St John's wort
* Pestle and mortar

Grind the pepper, rue and St John's wort together into a powder. Grind anti-clockwise while setting the intention to banish. This can be a laborious task, but as you work you will be infusing the blend with a strength of intent that matches your effort.

As you grind and blend the powder, fill this with your magickal intent and belief, and state the following:

"Gifts from earth, I ask of thee

From all that's bad, set me free,

I attract good energy,

As I will it, so mote it be."

Place the powder on the palm of your hand, take it outside, and blow it into the air – as you blow imagine that you are blowing all negativity into the wind, to be carried away forever.

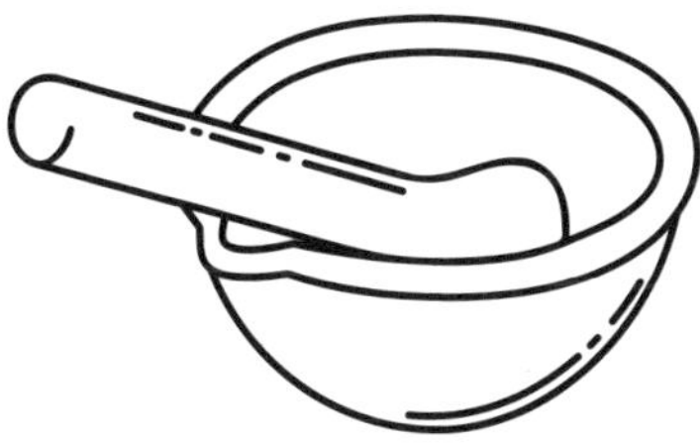

Cord Cutting

If you feel tied to a negative relationship, bad habits, or a situation or emotion that is draining and no longer serves you, a cord cutting ritual may be able to help.

This ritual should be done with no malice to anyone. Your intention here should never be harm, only to sever ties.

YOU WILL NEED:

* Fire-proof dish or tray
* Two black spell candles
* Length of string

At a time when you are feeling peaceful and calm, cleanse yourself and your space in whatever way aligns with your practice.

Stand your candles on the fire-proof tray using suitable candle holders, a couple of inches (about 5cm) apart. Tie them together with the string. Do this with the intention that one candle represents you, the other represents the person/emotion/thing you are separating yourself from.

Light the candles and state the following:

"As the cord is cut and the candles burned,

I cut all ties with that for which I yearned,

I release what no longer serves me,

As I will it, so mote it be."

Sit and meditate as the candles burn and the cord is cut and visualise your energetic attachment to the person/emotion/thing being cut. Feel yourself becoming detached, empowered and able to move on without this in your life.

BOUNDARY SETTING

Candle Spell for Setting Personal Boundaries

We must never feel selfish if we don't have the time or energy to just keep on giving of ourselves. It's important to be able to set boundaries and stick to them. Here's a candle spell to help you to do just that.

YOU WILL NEED:

* Small grey spell candle
* Dried rue
* Dried mint

Place the grey candle in a suitable holder, and circle it with the herbs, working clockwise.

As you light the candle, state the following:

"My boundaries will be clear,

I will set them without fear,

I will protect my energy

And choose only what's best for me."

As the candle burns down, feel yourself being empowered to say "no" when you'd like to, to communicate honestly and clearly, and know that moving forwards, you can do this without any feelings of guilt.

Doorway Candle Spell

A natural, calming, and protective candle spell to welcome loving vibrations into your home.

YOU WILL NEED:

* White candle

You may dress the candle with rose petals or rose oil to attract loving vibrations, but this is optional. Place the candle by your door to ensure only positive energy can enter. Light it and state this incantation:

"Negativity shall not cross my threshold,

Only loving vibrations may pass,

This is my command

And what I say, shall stand."

Protective Threshold Salt

A protective salt to keep negativity at bay.

YOU WILL NEED:

* Salt
* Basil
* Cinnamon

Add all the ingredients to a bowl, blending together counter-clockwise with intent to banish negativity and protect your home. Sprinkle your blend across the thresholds, stating:

"No evil shall cross into my space,

The line is drawn, and will remain in place,

Through wind and rain and the passing of time

My spell shall hold along this line."

This spell does not need to be repeated unless you feel the need.

Witches' Ladder Gate Charm

A beautiful, protective charm to hang on your gate to keep misfortune away.

YOU WILL NEED:

* Two or three lengths of string (equal in length)
* Dried lime slices
* Sprigs of rosemary
* Cinnamon sticks
* Root of ginger

Tie your pieces of string together and begin to braid them. Periodically stop to tie in the lime slices (you may need to create a hole in the slice to be able to thread this into your ladder), rosemary sprigs, and cinnamon sticks. Work mindfully and with firm intentions to create a protective charm. Repeat this until you are happy with the charm, then finish it off by tying in the ginger root for extra power. Your protective charm is now ready to hang.

Protect Your Home While You're Away

Here is some magick for when you are going away for a while and would like to offer your home (and anyone left behind) a little extra protection while you're gone.

YOU WILL NEED:

* Four black tourmaline crystals
* Iron nails
* Handful of salt

Sit with your crystals and set the intention that these magickal stones will protect your home. Place one crystal at each of the four corners of your home. If you have wooden doorframes, for extra protection, hammer an iron nail into the centre of the frames at your front and back doors. As you leave, take the handful of salt, walk away a little, turn around, and blow it with loving intent and protective energy towards the house.

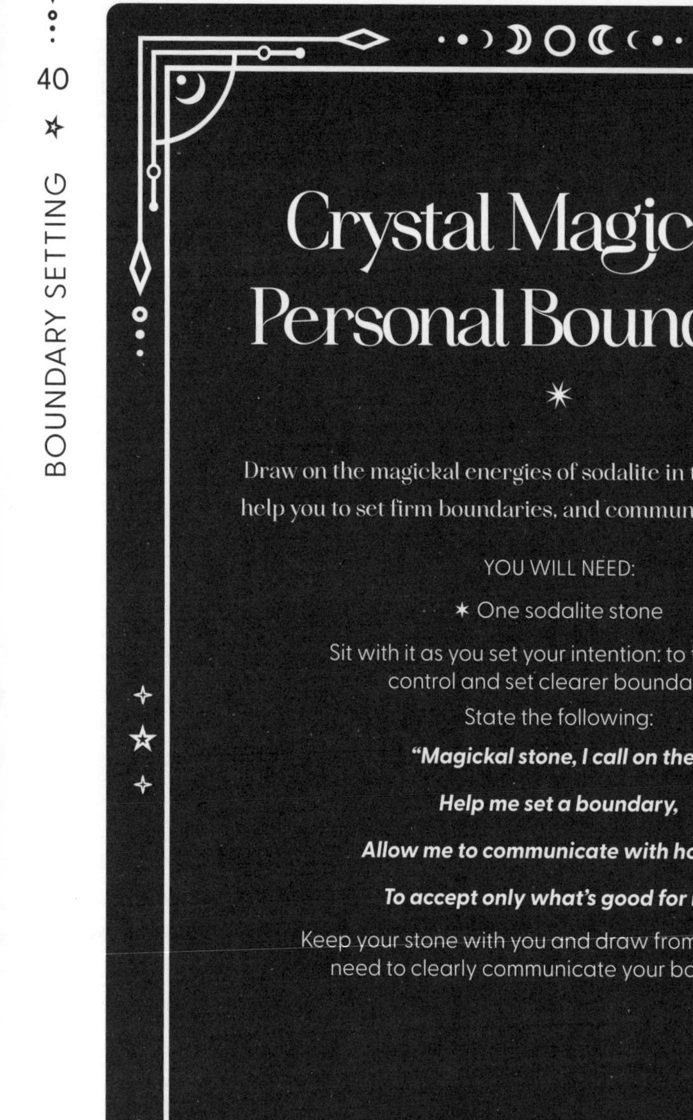

Crystal Magick for Personal Boundaries

Draw on the magickal energies of sodalite in this simple spell to help you to set firm boundaries, and communicate them clearly.

YOU WILL NEED:

* One sodalite stone

Sit with it as you set your intention: to take more control and set clearer boundaries.

State the following:

"Magickal stone, I call on thee

Help me set a boundary,

Allow me to communicate with honesty,

To accept only what's good for me."

Keep your stone with you and draw from it when you need to clearly communicate your boundaries.

Safe Home Spell Jar

A magickal jar to keep by your door to protect your home.

YOU WILL NEED:

* Small jar
* Bay leaves
* Salt
* Black pepper
* Onion skin
* Safety pin
* Black candle

Sit mindfully and add everything except for the safety pin and the candle to the jar, with intent.

Hold the safety pin in your hand and state the following:

"As I hold this pin in hand,

Safety is what I command."

Place the pin in the jar. Close the jar, and, holding the candle at an angle so the wax drips on the lid, seal it closed with black candle wax.

Keep your jar at the entrance to your home.

CLARITY

Know the Truth Candle Spell

A spell to bring clarity of mind by heightening your intuition.

YOU WILL NEED:

- Yarrow
- Lemon grass
- White spell candle

Blend the yarrow and lemon grass together clockwise, while setting your intention: to become more intuitive and have clarity of thought. Place your herb blend around the base of the candle working clockwise.

Light the candle, and as it burns state the following:

"Free my mind and open my eyes,

Let no thought be fogged by pride,

Third eye help me the truth to see,

As I will it, so mote it be."

Sit quietly and meditate as the candle burns down. Once your meditation is over trust in your instincts, visions, and dreams.

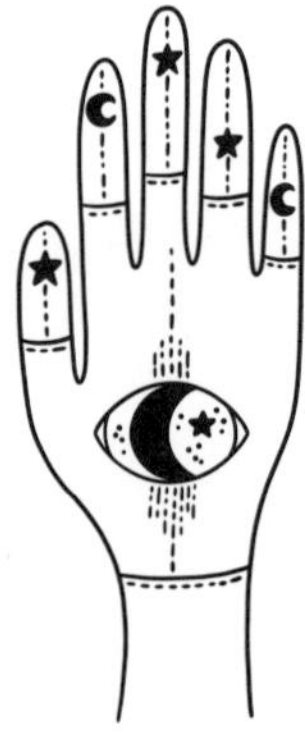

Water Spell for Clarity

Work with the magickal properties of water to aid clarity.

YOU WILL NEED:

- ✶ Bowl of water
- ✶ Clear quartz crystal

Place the clear quartz crystal in the bowl of water and think or say the following, while imagining the clarity of the water permeating through the quartz.

"My mind is clear, my eyes are open,

I find clarity in all words spoken,

Crystal clear shall leave no doubt,

The truth in all things shall jump right out."

Keep the quartz crystal with you.

Clarity Charm Bag

If you need to keep a clear head and not let muddled thinking cloud your judgement, keep a clarity charm bag with you.

YOU WILL NEED:

- ✶ Drawstring pouch
- ✶ Cloves
- ✶ Horehound
- ✶ Hematite stone
- ✶ Dried primrose

Add the items to the bag with firm intentions that this pouch will encourage clarity and lucidity. Draw the pouch tightly closed and keep it nearby.

Vase for Clear Thinking

This is a beautiful vase to encourage clarity of thought – place it wherever you study or work to keep a clear head.

YOU WILL NEED:

- Vase
- Fern
- Bluebells
- Primroses
- Rosemary

Fill a vase with the magickal plants listed above. As you work, incant the following:

"Energy from nature, ease my mind,

Muddled thoughts, I leave behind,

A clear head, I decree

From confusion, I am set free."

Divination for Clarity

If there is a particular issue you need clarity on, this divination ritual can help.

YOU WILL NEED:

- White candle
- Bowl of water (preferably moon water or rainwater)

Thinking about the situation for which you need clarity, and at a time when you feel completely relaxed, light the candle and tilt it so the wax drips into the bowl of water. Drop wax into the bowl until your intuition tells you it's enough. Then simply gaze into the bowl and seek answers in the shapes of the wax. If necessary, take the wax out of the bowl for a closer look. Remember that sometimes we 'sense' the answer in the shapes, more than we see it, so keep a very relaxed and open mind as you read the wax.

Clarity Witches' Brew

Matcha is known to encourage calmness and focus. Cacao is mind-opening and aids intuition. The two together make a powerful, earthy brew for clarity.

YOU WILL NEED:

- ½ tsp ceremonial grade matcha
- ½ tsp ceremonial grade cacao
- 1 cup (250ml) of your chosen plant milk

Heat the milk, then blend the matcha and the cacao into the milk – blend this very well, using a milk whisk for best results.

Sip mindfully, to relax and open your mind.

Clarity Glasses

Charm your spectacles to open your eyes and aid clear thinking.

Take some glasses and state the following while setting firm intentions:

"Enchanted glasses help me see

Not just what's in front of me,

Second-sight is what I need

So clarity is guaranteed."

CLEANSING

Floor Wash for Cleansing

Use the vibrations from Mother Nature to cleanse your floor and cleanse your space.

YOU WILL NEED:

* Warm water
* Salt
* Nettle
* Pine needles

Add salt to the warm water. Add the nettles and pine needles and allow them to steep.

Strain the water and use it to wash your hard floors; always washing from the inside, towards the door.

As you wash, state the following:

"Mother Nature cleanse my place,

Only good can enter this space.

Negative energy I expel

With this potent magick spell."

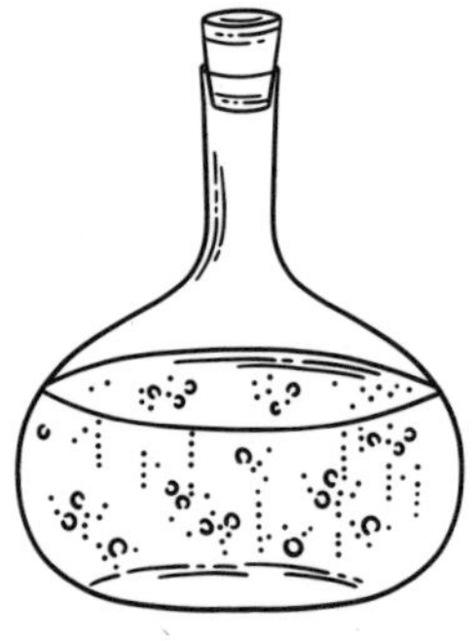

Lemongrass and Hawthorn Rice Bowl

A magickal bowl to grace your home, absorb negativity, and raise the vibrations of your surroundings.

YOU WILL NEED:

* Bowl
* Uncooked rice
* Dried lemongrass
* Dried hawthorn berries

Fill a bowl with uncooked rice. Add in some dried lemongrass and hawthorn berries to add extra potency.

Leave this bowl in a place you wish to have cleansed, and the rice bowl will absorb any negative energy from that space. Replace monthly, taking the old contents far from home to dispose of or bury them.

You may be surprised at how this simple cleansing bowl can remove so much negativity from your space and raise the vibration of your home.

Lime Shower Detox

A simple shower ritual to wash your negativity down the drain!

YOU WILL NEED:

* Half a lime

Take half a lime in the shower with you and wash with this instead of your usual soap.

As you rub the lime over your body, visualise your own negative energies and toxic thinking being washed down the drain with the juice from the lime. Once your feel completely cleansed, rinse your body with gratitude.

Simple House Blessing/Cleansing

A beautiful ritual to cleanse your home.

YOU WILL NEED:

* Incense

* Incenses, herbs, or resins chosen depending on your desired results, for example: **lavender** for calming, protecting and attracting peace and love; **dragon's blood** for banishing and protecting; **peppermint** to purify, calm, and heal; **sandalwood** for protecting and healing, and to attract serenity and peace; **frankincense** to protect and attract good fortune; and **cedar** to protect, purify, and heal

Clean and declutter – remove anything from your home that you feel gives off negative energy, and surround yourself with nice things that have a positive feel to them. Open all windows and doors and let the light and fresh air flood in! Don't forget to open all closets and drawers so you can be sure you have cleansed every space. When walking around your rooms, always start at the top of your home and work down. Walk counter-clockwise through each room (since counter-clockwise is the direction used to banish unwanted energy).

Light your incense, carrying it over something to catch the ash, and as you burn your chosen incense/herb/resin walk counter-clockwise through each room from top to bottom, blowing the smoke carefully into each corner and every cupboard. As you do so, state your intention (feel free to use your own words, or those below):

"Negative energies leave this space,

Love and light, take its place."

Once your cleansing ritual is complete, close all windows and doors and as you do so, again, state your intent:

"Only good may cross through here,

My space remains light and clear."

Your space is now cleansed!

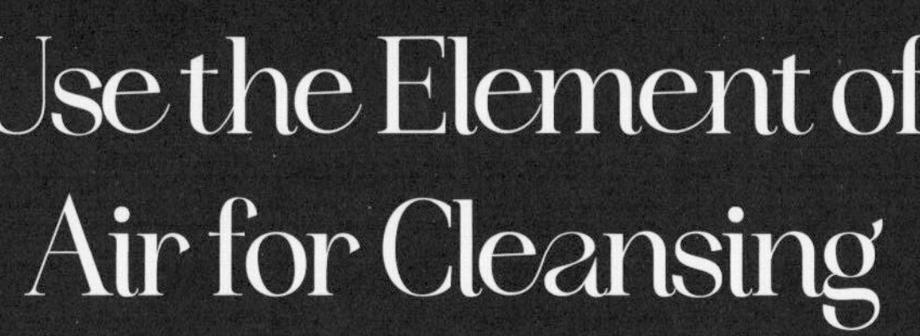

One of the easiest ways to cleanse your soul and remove stress and negativity.

Go outdoors on a windy day, stand mindfully, ground yourself, and set the intention that the wind will carry your stresses and anxieties away, and cleanse you of any negative energy. State the following:

"Air, carry away all that's wrong

Far away, I need it gone.

Thank you for cleansing me,

As I will it, so mote it be."

Aura Cleansing Spray

A cleansed aura helps us to make better decisions and behave in a more authentic way because our aura is no longer contaminated by the wants, needs, and emotions of others. Here is a magickal spray to cleanse your aura.

YOU WILL NEED:

* Moon water
* Rose essential oil
* Geranium essential oil
* Citronella essential oil

Blend a few drops of each of the essential oils together with the moon water, and add them to a spray bottle.

Spray a mist of this into the air and walk through it to cleanse your aura.

Cleansing Coffee

Add lavender to your morning coffee for a drink to empower, purify, and cleanse.

Add a sigil representing cleansing to your cup for extra potency.

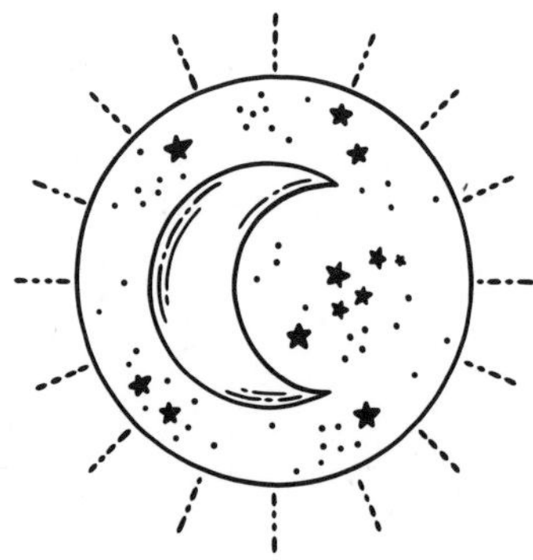

COURAGE & CONFIDENCE

Footwear for Courage

Make every step you take a confident one by enchanting your footwear!

As you put on your shoes/boots, state the following:

"I will walk with courage today,

Any fears shall slip away,

Magickal power, these shoes shall hold,

Each step I take, will be bold."

Confidence Witches' Brew

Raise your vibration and exude confidence with this magickal brew.

YOU WILL NEED:

* Moon water
* Ginger
* Yarrow

Boil the moon water and add the ginger and yarrow. Stir clockwise with intent and affirm:

"I have the confidence, charisma, and power to achieve my goals. I am an unstoppable force."

Steep for several minutes before straining. Once the brew is cool enough to sip, drink mindfully, and start to feel yourself exuding confidence – know that you are bold and strong, and can make it through anything the day holds for you.

Water for Calm Confidence

Water can be soothing but is also a force to be reckoned with!

YOU WILL NEED:

- Blue floating candle
- Eyebright
- Passionflower

Fill a bowl with water and stir in the eyebright and passionflower. Stir clockwise as you say the following:

"Calm of the lake,

Power of the ocean,

Manifest in me

As I stir this potion."

Float the candle in the bowl. Light it and meditate on it, feeling a sense of powerful calm inside you and surrounding you. Realise your power. When the flame has burned down, dispose of the candle. You can strain this potion and add it to your bath water.

Candle Spell for Courage

If you face a challenge that requires bravery, perform this spell beforehand to empower you and give you the courage you need.

YOU WILL NEED:

- Red spell candle
- Neroli oil
- Black pepper
- Tea leaves

Anoint the candle with the oil, working towards you to attract courage. Dress the candle in black pepper and tea leaves. Light it, and as it burns visualise yourself handling your challenge completely unphased. Then get out there and do it!

Summon Courage

Here's a simple ritual for you to perform when you feel overwhelmed and in need of courage.

YOU WILL NEED:

- Pen and paper
- Sharp object like a pin or darning needle
- Black or white spell candle
- Fire-proof dish

Note down on a piece of paper, the things you fear, the negative emotions you feel, and everything you would like to banish.

Take something sharp and etch into the candle sigils, symbols, etc. that represent courage to you.

Light the banishing black candle (you can use white as a substitute if you don't have black). In a fire-proof dish, burn the paper using the flame from the black candle to light it.

As the paper burns chant the following:

"Flames to make my fear choke,

All my doubts go up in smoke,

Courage fills my heart instead,

Bravery replaces dread."

Meditate on the black candle as it burns down, and feel yourself letting go of your fears and anxieties.

Take the ashes outside and bury them to signify that you've buried your fear.

Magickal Laundry Water

If you find yourself in need of confidence, or you need to command people's attention, washing your clothes beforehand using this magickal laundry water can help.

YOU WILL NEED:

* 1 cup (250ml) moon water
* Bergamot essential oil
* Cedar essential oil
* 1 tbsp dried rue

Add a few drops of each of the essential oils (bergamot for power, cedar for confidence) and the dried rue (for willpower) to the moon water. Pour into a lidded jar and leave it to steep overnight (if you can leave it in the moonlight, even better).

Then strain out the rue, leaving just the liquid, and add this to your laundry. As you dress, feel the powerful, commanding energy embrace you!

Courage Locket

A locket can be a perfect hidden charm to carry magick with you wherever you go.

YOU WILL NEED:

* Locket, or vial necklace
* Black cohosh
* Mustard seeds
* Black pepper

Place a tiny amount of each of the above in your locket or vial, with the intent to encourage bravery and confidence.

Wear this and clasp it in your hand to draw from its magickal energies when needed.

CREATIVITY

Creativity Charm Bag

This charm bag will help to alleviate mental blocks and encourage your creativity.

YOU WILL NEED:

* Blue drawstring pouch
* Horehound
* Birch
* Vervain
* Blue lace agate crystal

Blend your horehound, birch, and vervain clockwise while you focus your intent that these magickal herbs will encourage creativity. Focus on the area of your life in which you'd like to be more creative.

Hold your blue lace agate crystal and charge this with your intent. Chant the following, with gratitude that what you ask will be fulfilled:

"I call to thee, creativity,

It shall be as I decree,

Inspiration surrounding me,

Imagination is set free."

Add your herb blend and crystal to the charm bag; and feel free to add in anything else that you feel symbolises the type of creativity you seek.

Keep your charm bag close by.

Lapis Lazuli Meditation

Visualisation is a powerful aid to creativity, and so is meditation as it helps to relax the brain into a more creative state.

YOU WILL NEED:

* Lapis lazuli stone

Take the stone in your hand and sit or lie comfortably. Feel your body and mind becoming relaxed and open as you visualise yourself as the creative soul you wish to be. Imagine the energy from your powerful visualisation being absorbed into the stone.

Meditate for as long as it takes for you to feel that the stone is really charged with this creative energy. Now keep the stone with you and draw from its creative energy when needed.

Cacao Writing

Cacao helps to promote a state of relaxation and heightened focus, and is ideal for clearing mental blocks that hinder creativity.

YOU WILL NEED:

* Five orange tealights
* Cushion (to sit on)
* 1 cup ceremonial grade cacao
* Notepad and pen

Arrange your candles in a circle around the cushion you'll be sitting on. Light the candles with the intention that you are creating a circle of creativity.

Sit, relax, and drink your cacao mindfully while you think about the areas of your life that need your creativity. When you feel your mind becoming more relaxed and open, start to write down any ideas that come to mind. Maybe you'll feel the need to doodle or draw your ideas – just let your creative ideas flow onto the paper.

Creativity Pillow Pouch

This enchanting pouch will use the magickal properties of herbs and crystals to remove any creative blocks while you sleep.

YOU WILL NEED:

- Dried carnation petals
- Vervain
- Horehound
- Rainbow moonstone
- Drawstring pouch

Blend the carnation, vervain, and horehound together clockwise, setting the intention that they will attract creativity. Add them with the rainbow moonstone to the pouch, and tie it firmly closed. Place the pouch under your pillow to work its magick.

Creativity Bath

A gentle ritual to open the door to creativity.

YOU WILL NEED:

- Jasmine essential oil
- Peppermint essential oil
- Apatite crystal

Prepare yourself a warm bath and set the scene, if you wish, by using incense, candles, and music. Add a few drops of jasmine and peppermint essential oils and the apatite to your bath water. Swirl the water clockwise and state the following:

"As water flows so shall my creativity,

As I state it, it shall be."

As you envelop yourself in the water, inhale the aromas of the essential oils, and allow your mind to relax and open to allow creativity to flow.

Hanging Charm for Creativity

This magickal hanging charm will encourage creative energies into your space.

YOU WILL NEED:

* Pen and paper
* A length of string
* Sprig of lavender
* Sprig of violet flowers
* Stem of peppermint

Write down on the paper a list of things or projects you need help with, then roll the paper up towards you neatly.

Tie the paper in a bundle with the plants and hang this in your home, work, or magickal space as a charm to encourage creativity to flow.

Light the Spark Creativity Spell

✶

This beautiful fire ritual will symbolise how creativity can grow from a single spark.

YOU WILL NEED:

- ✶ Pen and paper
- ✶ A length of string
- ✶ Fire-proof bowl
- ✶ Orange spell candle

Write on the paper something about the area in your life or a project where you need to be more creative. Fold the paper towards you to attract creativity, tie it with string, then set it in the bowl. Light the orange candle, with the thought that this represents the first spark of creativity. Drip some of the orange wax onto the paper, then using the flame from the candle, light the paper and burn it.

State the following:

"My creativity grows like a fire from a spark,

Ideas and talent flow through me like the light breaks through the dark,

My creativity is unlocked, this fire holds the key,

This magickal fire represents the creativity that runs through me."

As the paper burns know that your creativity has been unlocked.

DIVINATION & THIRD EYE

Prophetic Dreams Candle Spell

Reveal hidden answers while you sleep!

YOU WILL NEED:

* Purple spell candle
* Jasmine flowers
* St John's wort
* Bay leaf
* Pen or pencil
* Length of string

Take your candle and place it in a suitable holder on a larger fire-proof surface.

Circle your candle with a blend of the jasmine flowers and St. John's wort, working clockwise.

Write your question on the bay leaf and wrap it round the candle, securing it with the string.

Light the candle and affirm:

"As I sleep, the truth be told,

In my dreams, it will unfold.

The truth will become clear to me,

As I will it, so mote it be."

As the candle burns, think about what it is you'd like insight into.

You can expect the bay leaf to spit a little when burned, so don't be alarmed'

Once the candle has burned out, you can sleep.

It is wise to keep a pen and paper beside your bed so that you can write down any insights and prophecies that come to you in your dreams.

Connecting to Spirit

A meditation ritual to allow you to connect to Spirit and gain insight into the unknown.

YOU WILL NEED:

- Pen and card
- White spell candle
- Cardamom seeds
- Marigold
- Yarrow flower

Do the following, with intent:

Write down the things you'd like insight into on the card.

Place the candle in a suitable holder or a heat-resistant dish.

Circle the candle with the cardamom seeds, marigold, and yarrow flower, working clockwise.

Sit with the card a while and think about the questions you'd like to have answered.

Then say the following:

"Spirit, I welcome thee,

Please bring the answers to me,

Give me insight, help me see,

As I will it, so mote it be."

Meditate as the candle burns, relax, and acknowledge the connection you are making to Spirit. Use your intuition... see what answers present themselves when you are in a meditative state. Finish by saying:

"Thank you, Spirit, for your insight and wisdom."

Divination Hand Wash

A magickal hand wash that can be used before divination such as tarot reading, runes, scrying, pendulum, etc. Or for use before spells such as those for prophetic dreams or third eye opening.

YOU WILL NEED:

- Moon water
- Cherry pits
- Lemon grass
- Dandelion root

Warm your moon water in a pan or cauldron. Steep your cherry pits, lemon grass, and dandelion root in the water for several minutes before straining. Give the herbs back to the earth with thanks. As you wash your hands in the warm, herb-infused moon water, state the following:

"Spirit, share your secrets with me,

Open my third eye, and let me see."

You are now ready for divination.

Divination Tool Wash

A simple wash to raise the vibration of your divination tools and make them more open to receive messages.

YOU WILL NEED:

- Eyebright
- Yarrow
- Water

Steep the eyebright and yarrow in water and place it outside during the full moon so it can be charged with the lunar energy.

The next day, strain the water. This water can be used to wipe down your divination table before card readings, or for cleansing your crystal ball, pendulum, etc.

Third Eye Bath

A magickal ritual for opening your third eye and preparing yourself for divination, prophetic dreams, etc.

YOU WILL NEED:

* Lavender flowers
* Cornflower petals
* 1 tbsp Epsom salt
* 1 tbsp coarse sea salt
* Jasmine essential oil

Blend everything together clockwise, setting your intention to open your third eye, heighten intuition, and enhance psychic abilities. Believe that you will see that which you desire to see. No more, no less.

Prepare yourself, and your bath or shower. This can mean meditating and grounding yourself, lighting candles, playing soft music, drinking herbal tea etc. It is helpful to do all that you can to prepare yourself and your ritual space, and make this a magickal experience.

The salt blend can then be added to a ritual bath, swirling clockwise. As the water soaks your body, feel all stress and tension washing away and allow the magickal blend to leave you feeling cleansed and refreshed. Feel your intuition heightening, and your third eye opening.

Third Eye Anointing Potion

This potion can be used to anoint candles, and any altar ware you are using in spells for opening the third eye, prophetic dreams, divination, etc.

YOU WILL NEED:

- Moon water
- Celery seeds
- Star anise

Add the moon water, celery seeds, and star anise to a pan or cauldron, and warm through.

As you stir clockwise, set your intentions, and affirm:

"A potion for psychic ability,

Answers will appear to me,

Third eye open so I can see

Wisdom that presents to me."

Allow the potion to cool, then strain. The potion is now ready to use.

Prophetic Dreams Pillow Pouch

Encourage insightful dreams by creating a magickal pillow pouch.

YOU WILL NEED:

- Pen and paper
- Purple drawstring pouch
- Violet (heartsease)
- Amethyst chips

Write your question or something you'd like insight into on your paper. Fold it towards you as many times as you can before placing it in the pouch.

Place the violet herb, and amethyst chips in your pouch and tie it firmly closed.

Sit with your pouch to set your intention – state the following:

"Charm, bring me knowledge tonight,

Show me answers, give insight.

With awareness, I shall be blessed,

Reveal the truth as I rest."

Place your pouch under your pillow, and see what insight comes to you in the night.

EMOTIONAL HEALING

Emotional Healing Bath Potion

This gentle healing potion can also be used as a foot soak, for those without a bathtub.

YOU WILL NEED:

- Moon water
- Carnation petals
- Orange blossoms
- Few drops of neroli essential oil

Add the carnation petals, orange blossoms, and neroli oil to your moon water. When your ritual bath is prepared, and your bathtub is full, gently pour your potion into the tub, and swirl your hands through the water in a clockwise direction, saying:

"I let go of pain which serves no purpose,

I release myself from damaging overthinking,

I am ready to take the positive from what has passed

And leave behind what is of no use to me,

I move forward with positivity."

As you soak in your magickal waters, open yourself up to healing and allow yourself to release any pent-up emotions that you have been burying. Feel them, process them, and let them go! This can be a painful experience, but it is important for your healing to accept and feel emotions, before releasing them.

Two Elements for Emotional Healing

A beautiful healing ritual incorporating the power of fire and the healing energy of water.

YOU WILL NEED:

* Lavender
* Yarrow flower
* White floating candle
* Cucumber slices

Fill a bowl with water and stir in the lavender and yarrow flower. Stir clockwise as you say the following:

"Lavender and yarrow flower,

Imbue this water with healing power."

Set the floating candle in the bowl and float the slices of cucumber around it.

Light the candle as you say the following:

"Powerful healing I invoke

By the power of fire and smoke."

Meditate on the flame and feel a sense of powerful healing surrounding you. Feel this healing flowing through you and know that you are safe and loved and embraced by magick.

Once the flame has burned down, you may dispose of the candle and return the cucumber and flowers to the earth with thanks.

You can also use the water for a ritual bath by straining out the herbs and adding the potion to your bath water.

Emotional Healing Aura Spray

An aura spray to raise your vibration and attract healing energies.

YOU WILL NEED:

* 1 cup (250ml) distilled water
* Rose hips
* Lavender
* Rose quartz crystal chips
* Spray bottle

If you need to preserve this spray so it lasts more than a few days, then you can work with 50% distilled water and add 50% witch hazel or alcohol as a preservative.

Add the distilled water to a pan. Heat it through (there's no need to boil it, warm water is fine), then add the lavender and rose hips to the pan. Stir the water clockwise and charge it with the intention that this magickal blend will bring healing. State the following:

"Mother Nature, I thank thee

For your magickal energy

And healing that you bring to me,

As I will it, so mote it be."

Allow to cool. Strain the water, setting the lavender and rose hips aside (this can be given back to nature with thanks, as its purpose has been served). Add a couple of crystal chips to an atomiser or spray bottle, and add the magickally infused water. Spray this around you to raise your vibration and encourage healing.

Emotional Healing Candle Spell

A gentle spell to soothe and heal.

YOU WILL NEED:

- White spell candle
- Few drops each of jasmine, rose, and lavender essential oils

Mindfully blend the oils together clockwise. Anoint the candle, towards you to attract healing, then light it, and say:

"Healing flame, pure and bright

Take heavy burdens, and make them light,

All things passed are lessons learned,

Negativity, in your flame be burned."

Meditate as the candle burns, knowing that you may heal, move forwards, and be at peace with all that has passed.

Heart Healing Witches' Brew

A mindful blend to sooth your heart and lift your spirits.

YOU WILL NEED:

- Moon water
- Peppermint
- Apple slices
- Dried dandelion

Add the ingredients to boiling moon water. Stir clockwise with intent and affirm:

"I nurture my soul and heal my heart with these magickal gifts from Mother Nature."

Steep for several minutes before straining. Return the plant material to the earth with thanks. Once the brew is cool enough to sip, drink mindfully, and feel your soul being nourished.

Heart-Healing Bath Salts

This magickal recipe is ideal when you just need to soak for a while and wash away the past, welcome the future, and heal your heart.

YOU WILL NEED:

- ¼ cup (75g) Epsom salts
- ¼ cup (75g) coarse sea salt
- Rose petals
- Chamomile
- Few drops of sandalwood essential oil

Blend the ingredients together, clockwise to attract healing, and set the intention that the salts will heal your heart and help you to move forwards.

Set the mood for your bath in whatever way suits you – your chosen music, candles, etc. Add the salts to your bath, swirling clockwise.

Then, as you bathe in your magickal salt bath, embrace positive thoughts, imagine your life moving forwards with joy, and feel the magickal salts washing away negativity, welcoming joy, and healing your heart.

Open your Heart Bath Pouch

A beautiful ritual to help to heal and open your heart. It can also be used as a foot soak, or you can hang the bath pouch over your shower head if you don't have a bath.

YOU WILL NEED:

- Rose petals
- Lemon balm
- Apricot pit
- Drawstring pouch
- Pink tealight

At a time when you can be relaxed and undisturbed, add your rose petals, lemon balm, and apricot pit to the bath pouch.

Run yourself a luxuriously warm bath, light the pink candle, and set the mood for peace. As you add the pouch to your water, swirl the water clockwise and state the following:

"Magickal waters heal my heart and mind

And prepare me for receiving the love I desire.

Love will surround me in abundance

And I am ready and open to receive it,

As I will it, so mote it be."

As you bathe, feel the magickal waters enveloping you and soothing your heart and soul, opening your heart with optimism and trust, and readying you for the love that is on its way.

EMPOWERMENT

Empowerment Charm Bag

A magickal pouch to carry with you to empower you.

YOU WILL NEED:

- ✶ Mountain ash berries
- ✶ Eyebright
- ✶ Blue cohosh
- ✶ Red jasper
- ✶ Red drawstring pouch

Blend the mountain ash berries, eyebright, and blue cohosh together clockwise, setting the intention that their magickal properties will empower you.

Sit with the red jasper and charge it with your energy.

Add the blend together with the red jasper to your pouch and tie it firmly closed.

Sit with your pouch and meditate.

Visualise your more powerful, confident self – feel yourself becoming stronger and more empowered as you draw from the magickal properties of your charm.

Keep the pouch close by and draw from its empowering energy when needed.

Empowerment Spell Bottle

A magickal bottle to keep in your home, on your altar, your desk, or anywhere where you like to feel more empowered.

YOU WILL NEED:

* Dried fennel, calendula, and honeysuckle
* Small bottle with lid
* Orange candle
* Clear quartz crystal

Add the herbs and honeysuckle to the bottle and say:

"Calendula bring respect to me,

Fennel for vitality,

Honeysuckle for tenacity,

Together to empower me,

As I will it, so mote it be."

Place the lid on the bottle. Light your candle and, holding it at an angle, drip some wax around the bottle top to seal it. While the wax is still liquid, add a quartz crystal to the top of your bottle.

Empowering Ritual Bath

A very simple ritual bath to energise and empower.

YOU WILL NEED:

* Ylang ylang and neroli essential oils
* White spell candles

Run a warm bath and add a few drops of each oil to the water. Light the white candles, safely, around the bath. As you bathe, breathe deeply the aroma from your magickal waters, and feel yourself growing more empowered. Feel your vitality increasing, and your confidence growing. Know that these waters are washing away insecurity and self-doubt.

Empowerment Spell Powder

Create a magickal powder to use in spells and rituals for empowerment.

YOU WILL NEED:

- Yarrow
- Bay leaves
- Caraway seeds
- Mint
- Pestle and mortar

Grind the herbs and yarrow together, clockwise, into a powder. Do this with intent to empower. This can be a laborious task, but as you work you will be infusing the herbs with the power of your strong intentions. As you grind and blend the powder, infuse it with your magickal intent and belief, and state the following:

"Nature's power I add to thee,

Powder potent as can be

Attracting strength and energy

To anything that I decree."

Here are just a few ways to use powders in your spell work:

Blowing: Place the powder on the palm of your hand and blow it into the air. If casting a spell to empower someone else, even if that person is far away, you should blow in their direction.

Drawing: You can draw with your powder to mark out a circle for rituals, to make magickal patterns or sigils on the altar, or to mark out visually the intentions of a spell.

Dressing: You can dress items with spell powder, such as ritual candles, letters, business cards, money, or application forms.

Wearing: You can wear your powder like a talc (assuming you are not allergic or sensitive to the ingredients) or add it to charm bags etc. Wearing the powder is a good way of taking the magick with you to important meetings, events, or rituals.

Empowering Witches' Brew

Give yourself energy and powerful vibrations with this delicious witches' brew.

YOU WILL NEED:

- Cinnamon
- Ginger
- Sunflower petals
- Tea infuser
- Moon water

Add the above to your tea infuser and allow to infuse in hot (previously boiled) moon water.

Swirl the infuser clockwise in your cup with intent.

Leave to steep for five minutes, the remove the infuser, and once the brew is cool enough, sip mindfully.

Feel yourself being filled by lunar energy and the empowering vibrations of the plants.

Empowerment Candle Spell

This is the spell for you if you have an event or occasion coming up, or something specific that you must manage, which you need to empower yourself to overcome. Perform this ritual at the time you need to be empowered.

YOU WILL NEED:

- Piece of paper and pencil
- Red spell candle
- Length of string
- Candle holder
- Fire-proof bowl
- Salt

Write on the piece of paper exactly what you need to be empowered to overcome. Wrap the paper round the spell candle and tie it with string.

Place the candle in a candle holder and place the holder in the bowl. Surround it with salt.

Light the candle, and as it burns, state the following:

"Fire, I call on thee,

Surround me with your energy,

Burning flame, empower me,

As I will it, so mote it be."

As the candle burns, feel yourself being imbued with power.

Find Your Inner Strength

A simple, beautiful ritual to make you realise the strength that you hold.

Light a red spell candle.
Stand in front of it and, raising your arms, express your power as follows:

"Hear me, as I decree

There is a great power inside of me.

I shall not be diminished, I shall not reduce,

An authentic life is what I choose.

I take the power in my hands,

Energy from the air and from the land,

A perfect storm I brew in me

To call upon in times of need.

My magick I wield like a mighty sword

To cut negativity like a cord,

Ancestral power handed down

Bestowed on me, like the family crown.

I am a loving, magickal, and yet fierce soul,

Unbroken, I am powerful, and whole."

FORGIVENESS & LETTING GO

Forgiveness Charm Bag

Forgiveness is the kindest thing we can do for ourselves, as harbouring bad-feeling, resentment, or anger, is bad for our souls and lowers our vibration. Here's a beautiful charm bag to help with forgiveness.

YOU WILL NEED:

* Small piece of paper and pen
* Blue drawstring pouch
* Cornflowers
* Rose petals
* Amethyst crystal

Sit for a moment and consider who you'd like to forgive, whether it's yourself or someone else. Don't dwell on what they did to you, but think about how free you will feel once you have processed your feelings and moved on with forgiveness.

Take the paper and note down an affirmation like "I forgive", or something that resonates with you.

Add this to the pouch with the cornflowers, rose petals, and amethyst, and tie the pouch closed.

Sit with your pouch and affirm:

"Forgiveness, it shall set me free,

As I will it, so mote it be."

When you feel the need, sit with your drawstring pouch and meditate. Process your emotions, and gradually you will feel able to forgive.

Once you feel that it no longer serves, you can empty the pouch, return the herbs to the earth with thanks, and cleanse amethyst for re-use.

Waning Moon Letting Go Ritual

The waning moon is a great time for letting go, and here's a ritual to help you to do just that.

YOU WILL NEED:

- Marjoram
- Lemon balm
- Black pepper
- White spell candle
- Paper and pencil
- Fire-proof dish

Choose a date when the moon is waning for this ritual. Blend the marjoram, lemon balm, and pepper, stirring counter-clockwise with the intention to banish and let go of anything that no longer serves you.

Place the candle in a suitable holder and encircle it counter-clockwise with the herb blend.

Light the candle, and as it burns, note down all the things you wish to let go of.

Ensuring you have a fire-proof dish ready, safely burn the paper, and feel the release as you see those things go up in smoke. Feel yourself becoming unburdened and lighter, and feel gratitude as you now meditate on the burning candle flame.

When your ritual is complete, dispose of the ashes and herbs, ensuring the ashes are taken far from home or buried deep – signifying that those things you wanted gone, will stay gone!

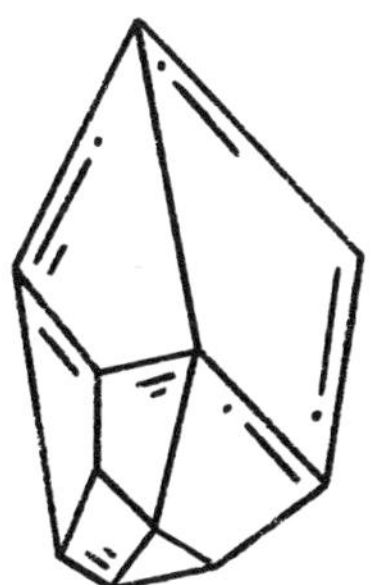

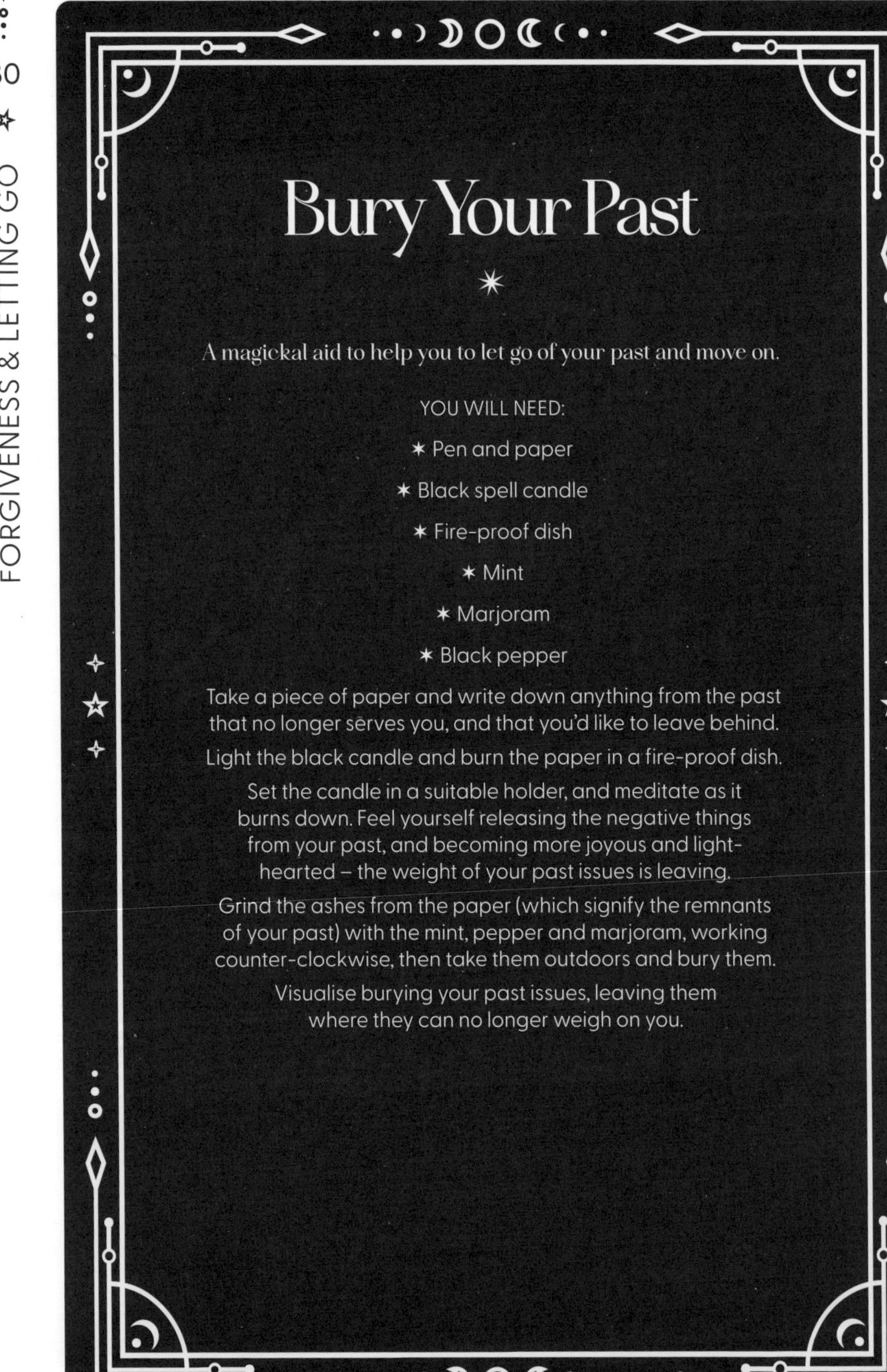

Bury Your Past

A magickal aid to help you to let go of your past and move on.

YOU WILL NEED:

- Pen and paper
- Black spell candle
- Fire-proof dish
- Mint
- Marjoram
- Black pepper

Take a piece of paper and write down anything from the past that no longer serves you, and that you'd like to leave behind.

Light the black candle and burn the paper in a fire-proof dish.

Set the candle in a suitable holder, and meditate as it burns down. Feel yourself releasing the negative things from your past, and becoming more joyous and light-hearted – the weight of your past issues is leaving.

Grind the ashes from the paper (which signify the remnants of your past) with the mint, pepper and marjoram, working counter-clockwise, then take them outdoors and bury them.

Visualise burying your past issues, leaving them where they can no longer weigh on you.

Forgiveness Candle Rite

A gentle ritual to open the heart and encourage forgiveness.

YOU WILL NEED:

- Half an orange
- Pale blue spell candle
- Rosemary
- Lemon balm
- Rose petals

Place your half an orange on a plate, flesh side up. You may wish to chop the base off, so it sits without wobbling. Push your candle into the orange so you are effectively using the orange as a candle holder.

Sprinkle the rosemary, lemon balm, and rose petals over the orange clockwise with intent to attract forgiveness. Light the candle and meditate, feel bitterness, anger, and sorrow ebbing away as the candle burns down.

Stone Casting Letting Go

A simple yet powerful ritual to let go, and move on.

YOU WILL NEED:

- Pebble

Take your pebble in your hand and sit with it.

Take some time to sit quietly and give your worries, stresses, and negative emotions to the pebble. You can think, or say out loud, the things you'd like to let go of, and move on from.

Take your pebble to a natural body of water, like a lake, river, or ocean, and cast it into the water. Know as you walk away with gratitude that your troubles are being washed away. If you don't have access to a natural body of water, the alternative is to take your pebble away from your home and bury it.

GOOD FORTUNE

Good Luck Charm Bag

Create a magickal pouch to turn your luck around and attract good fortune.

YOU WILL NEED:

* Blue violet
* Dried orange peel
* Strawberry leaf
* Citrine crystal
* Green drawstring pouch
* Embroidery needle and white thread

Sit quietly with each of the above items and set your intention: to attract good luck.

Add the blue violet, dried orange peel, strawberry leaf, and crystal to your pouch and tie it firmly closed. Embroider an arrow sigil onto your pouch while saying the following:

"Like an arrow, at highest speed,

Attract to me what I need,

A charm to keep bad luck at bay

And bring good fortune right away."

Keep your charm bag close by and reset your intention as often as you feel it is needed.

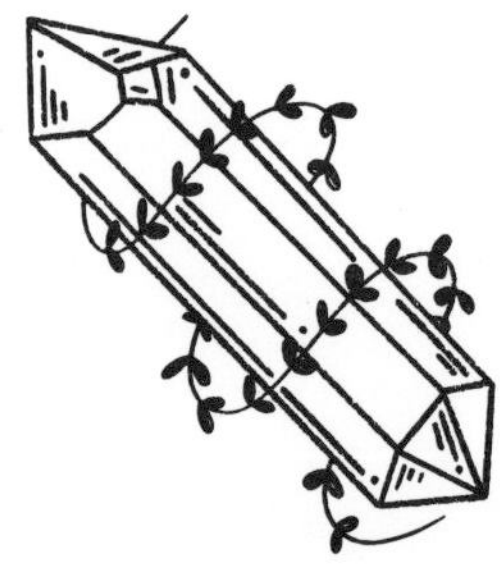

Good Fortune Simmering Pot

An enchanting simmer pot to fill your home with abundant vibrations and attract good fortune.

YOU WILL NEED:

* Jasmine
* Chamomile
* Orange peel
* Pineapple
* Moon water

Add all the ingredients to a pan or cauldron of water (at least a little of this should be moon water), stir clockwise and say:

"Magickal pot empowered by the moon

Fill my home with good fortune,

As my blessings come to me

Gratitude I give to thee."

Heat to a simmer.

Allow your pot to simmer gently so the aromas and vibrations from your pot permeate through your home.

Good Fortune Body Spray

Attract luck wherever you go by using a body spray designed to attract good fortune your way!

YOU WILL NEED:

* 1½fl oz (50ml) jojoba oil
* A few drops of violet, bergamot, and lavender essential oils

With intentions set, add a few drops of each of the essential oils to the jojoba oil. Add the liquid to a spray bottle or atomiser and use this to spray your body and aura, and encourage good fortune to come your way.

Good Fortune Threshold Wash

Make a magickal wash to ensure only good fortune enters your home.

YOU WILL NEED:

- Salt
- Vinegar
- Rose hips
- Chamomile
- Green aventurine or citrine crystal

Add a little salt, the rose hips, chamomile, crystal, and vinegar to a pan or cauldron of warm water. Stir clockwise to attract, and affirm:

"Good fortune come to me

In abundance, I decree,

Luck will flow fast and free,

As I will it, so mote it be."

Strain the water and return the plants to the earth with thanks. The crystal can be cleansed for future use. Wash your doorways, doors, and window frames, and know that good luck is headed swiftly to you and your home, and that fortune is smiling on you!

Incantation for Good Fortune

Take any item in your hand and state the following with intent to turn it into a magickal good luck charm.

"A charm to attract good luck my way

And keep all misfortune at bay,

Directly to me blessings shall come,

This is my spell; it shall be done."

Turnaround Candle Spell

A beautiful candle spell to turn your luck around, banish misfortune and attract good fortune.

YOU WILL NEED:

- 1 pineapple
- White spell candle
- Salt
- Ground cinnamon

Slice your pineapple in half and place your candle in the bottom half of the pineapple to use the pineapple as a candle holder. Encircle the candle by sprinkling the salt on the pineapple around the candle in a counter-clockwise motion.

State the following:

"Misfortune and negativity, I cast you out."

Next sprinkle the cinnamon powder in a circle on top of the salt, this time clockwise, and state something like:

"Good fortune come about."

Light your candle. As it burns, visualise all misfortune melting away and leaving your body, mind, and home, and welcome in positivity and good fortune.

As you visualise your luck being turned around, feel nothing but gratitude as your candle burns out.

Horseshoe Door Charm

Make a pretty and magickal charm to place on your door to attract good luck to you household.

YOU WILL NEED:

* Crafting wire
* Needle and thread
* Dried orange slices
* Oak leaves
* Cinnamon sticks
* Dried heather
* Dried camomile stems

Working mindfully with intent and gratitude for the good luck you are manifesting, twist lengths of crafting wire together to make a thick, sturdy horseshoe shape.

Decorate your horseshoe by sewing in dried orange, oak leaves, and cinnamon sticks, and weaving in the heather and chamomile until you are happy that your charm is filled with magick.

Once you have finished your decorative charm, hang it on the door of your home to attract good luck. Ensure the horseshoe is hung with the ends pointing upwards.

GRATITUDE

Daily Gratitude

This is a ritual to encourage you to show gratitude every day – and in doing so, manifest good fortune.

YOU WILL NEED:

* Pen and paper
* Small white spell candle

Each day, for seven days, note down the things you are grateful for. These can be small things, like that perfect brew you had this morning, or large things like getting the keys to your new home – the point is to find a few things each day and be truly grateful for them. As you note them down, reflect on the joy these things bring you.

On the seventh day, light your white spell candle and state the following:

"I send out joy and gratitude for my blessings this week, and I attract more blessings in the weeks ahead. As I will it, so mote it be."

Sit with your paper as the candle burns and meditate on all the things you are grateful for.

Once the candle has burned out, your spell is complete.

Gratitude Bath Potion

Take a bath and count your blessings!

YOU WILL NEED:

* Orange peel
* Rose petals
* Rose quartz
* Moon water

Add the orange peel, rose petals, and rose quartz to your moon water. When your ritual bath is prepared, and your bathtub is full, gently pour your potion into the tub, and swirl your hands through the water in a clockwise direction, stating the following:

"I am grateful each day for the blessings in my life.

I am at one with Spirit, and know my needs will always be recognised."

As you soak in your magickal waters, think about your blessings, acknowledge all the things you are grateful for, and know that in giving thanks and recognising your blessings, you will attract even more beautiful things into your life.

Bright Blessings Bath or Shower Pouch

A lovely ritual to help you appreciate your blessings.

YOU WILL NEED:

* Drawstring pouch
* Chamomile
* Rose petals
* Sunflower petals

Chamomile and rose petals are both renowned for their soothing, loving properties. They help us to notice our blessings and encourage gratitude. Sunflowers promote peace and joy.

Sit quietly, and mindfully add the chamomile, rose petals, and sunflower petals to the bath pouch. Do so with gratitude for the blessings this magickal pouch will remind you of, then you can tie the pouch closed.

Prepare yourself a bath and add the pouch to the water. As you soak in the water's magickal properties, remind yourself of all the ways, big and small, that you are blessed. Do not allow any negative thoughts to linger. Give gratitude and relax.

If you don't have a bath, the pouch can be hung over your showerhead, or added to a foot soak.

Gratitude Candle Spell

Light a candle and send your gratitude out into the Universe. The more you recognise your blessings and give thanks for them, then the more blessings will be attracted to you.

YOU WILL NEED

* White spell candle
* Sharp tool like a pin or darning needle

Etch sigils into the candle using your sharp tool – be creative and draw whatever sigils feel right to you. Or you can simply etch "thank you", or "gratitude". As you do this think of the things you are thankful for, and work mindfully, with intent.

Light the candle and state the following:

"Gratitude I give to thee,

I send you loving energy."

As your candle burns your gratitude is being sent into the Universe.

Apple for Gratitude

Take an apple and put your athame through the centre of it. Push it deep inside the apple, but don't allow it to pierce the skin on the bottom.

Use your athame to direct your gratitude into the apple. Think of your blessings, feel the gratitude, then channel it through your athame and into the apple.

Now cut the apple in half. One half will be for you, and the other an offering for the universe.

Eat your half and feel the nourishment from the fruit, again, feeling gratitude.

Take the other half and plant it outdoors as an offering to nature, the Universe, or whatever deity you worship.

Gratitude Beads

The principal of gratitude beads is a simple one – the longer your thread, the better! Gratitude is a spell of its own that encourages more blessings.

YOU WILL NEED:

* Strong thread
* Beads made from natural materials: wood, stone, or crystal

Whenever you are blessed with good fortune – time spent with a friend, good conversation, a gift, a beautiful walk in nature, or anything else that deserves your gratitude – sit with a bead and think about this blessing before threading the bead on the thread. The aim is to create a long string of beads. As it grows you can use it as a meditation aid, a hanging charm in your home, a necklace, or a garland to hang over your altar. Each time you look at it, you will be reminded of your many blessings.

Gratitude Bowl

This beautiful bowl is a reminder to count your blessings daily.

Start by adding a layer of sand to the bottom of a bowl.

Each time something good happens that you are grateful for, add something beautiful to the bowl. This could be a dried flower, a pretty stone, an acorn, a little note, or whatever feels right to you. Be thankful and add to your bowl for small things too – grow your gratitude bowl into something beautiful.

This bowl can be something to focus on when times aren't so great, to remind you of the blessings in your life.

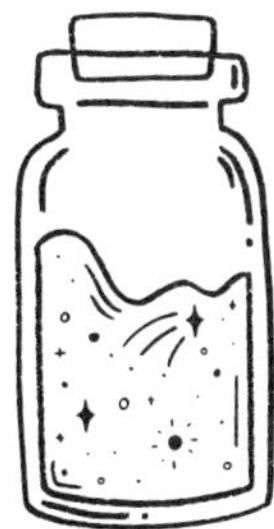

HAPPINESS

Happiness Bath

A relaxing ritual to encourage positivity and joy.

YOU WILL NEED:

* Rose petals
* Lavender
* Neroli essential oil

Prepare yourself a nice relaxing bath. Set the mood as you desire with your choice of incense, candles, and/or music (optional). Add the rose petals, lavender, and a few drops of neroli oil to your bathwater. As you bathe, allow the magickal herbs to wash away all sorrow and negativity. As you wash, state the following:

"Magickal waters wash away sadness

And fill my soul with joy and gladness."

Mood-Lifting Smelling Salts

If you feel low energy and low vibrations, and could use an instant lift, these mood-lifting smelling salts are the answer.

YOU WILL NEED:

* Epsom salts
* Coarse sea salt
* Neroli, ylang ylang, and rose essential oils

Blend together equal parts Epsom salts and sea salt. Add several drops of each essential oil and blend clockwise with intent, to attract happiness. Keep the magickal salt in a sealed pot and breathe in the aroma to give you a lift when you're feeling down.

This can also be used as a mood-lifting bath salt or foot soak.

Happy Home Boundary Powder

A magickal powder to attract happiness to your home.

YOU WILL NEED:

- Strawberry leaves
- Marjoram
- Oregano
- Pestle and mortar

Grind the strawberry leaves, marjoram, and oregano clockwise with intent to attract happiness. Grind until it becomes a fine powder – this will take time and energy, but the more time and work you put into this, the more powerful the magick will be.

Scatter this clockwise around the perimeter of your home with the intent to attract joy.

Happiness Room Spray

Spray this magickal blend lightly around your home to raise the vibration and create a more joyous atmosphere!

YOU WILL NEED:

- Moon water
- Neroli essential oil
- Rose essential oil
- Three cherry pits
- Small sunstone crystal

Add a few drops each of the neroli and rose oils and the cherry pits and crystal to your moon water. Blend this clockwise with intention set that this blend will attract happiness.

Add to a spray bottle and spritz lightly around your home to attract joy.

Happy Home Floor Wash

Raise the vibrations of your home by washing your floor with this magickal wash.

YOU WILL NEED:

* Salt
* Rose petals
* Oregano
* Lavender essential oil
* Vinegar

Add a little salt, some rose petals, oregano, lavender oil, and vinegar to a pan or cauldron of warm water. Stir clockwise to attract gladness, and affirm:

"Happy home, filled with joy,

This is my desire.

Mother nature, and her gifts,

Will raise vibrations higher."

Strain the water and return the herbs to the earth with thanks.

Wash your floors working from the inside, towards the door, and feel the joy entering your home and your soul – be sure to inject your own positivity into the cleansing, and know that the joy you give out will come back to you and fill your home with happiness!

A Garland of Joy

This is a decorative garland that will encourage joy into your home.

YOU WILL NEED:

- Needle and strong thread
- Dried orange slices
- Cinnamon sticks
- Dried roses
- Star anise

Attach the above items to your thread, working mindfully and with a joyous heart. Some of the items can be tied on, and some may be easier to sew on.

Alternate and repeat the items until you have a nice decorative length for a garland.

Hang it in your home to attract joy.

Happiness Charm Bag

This charm bag is best created while you have a positive mindset, since the energy you put into it is all important.

YOU WILL NEED:

* Star anise
* Marigold
* Sunstone
* Gold or white drawstring pouch

Blend the star anise and marigold together clockwise, setting your intention: to create a blend full of positive energy and joy.

Sit with your sunstone and meditate with it, visualising the joy you hope to achieve.

Add your blend and sunstone to the pouch.

Feel free to add in anything else you feel is right, from affirmations to amulets. This is your charm bag, so it's okay to make it personal to you, although this is optional.

Tie the pouch closed. Keep it with you when you feel you need to draw from its positive energy.

Recharge and re-use as needed.

HEALING

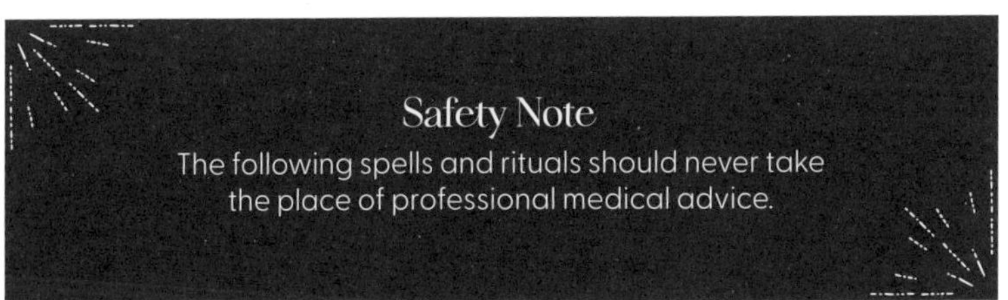

Healing Charm Bag

A charm to help with emotional or physical healing.

YOU WILL NEED:

- White drawstring pouch
- Blackberry leaves
- Chamomile
- Dried carnation petals

Add the items to your pouch while setting your intention: that this charm bag will bring healing energy to its bearer.

You can also add in notes like “my anxiety is healed” or “my heartache is healed”, or whatever relates to the specific healing you need. You can also include talismans, amulets, or other items that resonate with you, but this is optional.

Then close the bag and tie it firmly closed.

Keep the bag close by and draw from its healing energy.

Distance Healing Spell Powder

Here is a very useful spell for when you wish to send healing to someone who lives far away.

YOU WILL NEED:

* Fennel seeds
* Barley
* Rosemary
* Lavender
* Pestle and mortar

Grind your herbs down into a fine powder – think about the person you are wishing to heal and imagine them on the mend and feeling better. This is a laborious task, but the spell will be better served the more intention and effort you put into it.

Take your powder outdoors and blow it in the direction of the person you are hoping to heal. It doesn't matter if this person is thousands of miles away; you are setting your intention to heal with the act of blowing. State the following:

"I call upon the element of air

To carry healing with loving care.

I send my healing energy with thee,

As I will it, so mote it be."

Thank the elements of earth and air for helping you with your magick. Your spell is complete.

Healing Anointing Potion

This potion can be used to anoint candles and any altar ware you are using in spells for healing.

YOU WILL NEED:

* Moon water
* Lavender
* Chamomile
* Eucalyptus

Add the moon water, lavender, chamomile, and eucalyptus to a pan or cauldron, and warm through. As you stir clockwise to promote healing, set your intentions, and affirm:

"Healing intent I add to thee,

Pain and hurt be gone,

Peace and relief take its place,

Suffering be done."

Allow the potion to cool, then strain out the plants (these can be returned to the earth with thanks). The potion is now ready.

Healing Candle Spell

A beautiful ritual of healing for yourself or a loved one.

YOU WILL NEED:

* Photograph of the person you wish to heal
* Dried peppermint
* Yarrow flower
* Barley
* Blue spell candle

Surround the photograph with peppermint, yarrow flower, and barley, working clockwise to attract healing. Charge the candle with your intent to heal and place it in front of the photograph.

Light the candle and as it burns visualise your desired outcome; see yourself or your loved one feeling happy and healed, and feel gratitude that this will be manifested. Leave the photograph and herbs in place until you feel the spell no longer serves.

Physical Healing Aromatherapy Pillow

This magickal aromatherapy blend will help to build resilience to sickness, and enhance determination and the will to heal.

YOU WILL NEED:

* Two equal squares of fabric, about 4in (10cm) square
* Needle and thread
* Eucalyptus
* Peppermint
* Lavender

Placing the two pieces of fabric on top of one another, mindfully sew the edges of the fabric together, leaving an opening so you can fill your pillow. Fill the pillow with the eucalyptus, peppermint, and lavender, then sew closed. Sit with the pillow and charge it with your own healing energy before placing it under the pillow of the person in need of healing.

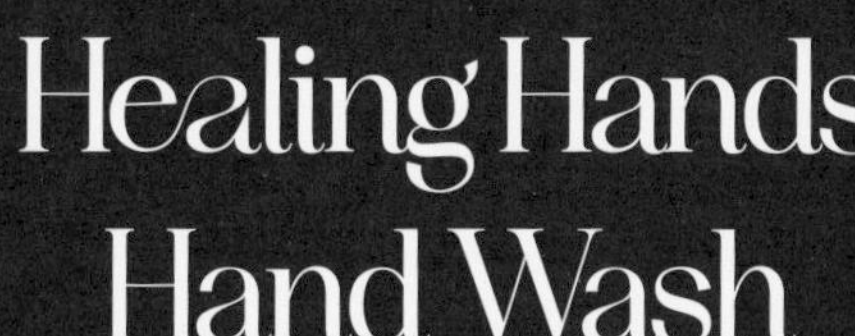

Healing Hands Hand Wash

This hand wash can be used before you physically care for someone who is sick or injured, or before you give a massage. It is also good to use before you practice reiki or perform any kind of healing spell or ritual.

YOU WILL NEED:

- Moon water
- Apple
- Ginseng
- Rosemary

Warm your moon water in a pan or cauldron.

Steep your apple, ginseng, and rosemary in the water for several minutes before straining.

As you wash your hands in the warm, plant-infused moon water, state the following:

"Healing hands serve me well,

Draw energy from this magick spell,

This wash I use will bring to me

Magickal, healing energy."

You are now ready for healing magick.

Healing Witches' Brew

Fill yourself with the healing energies of this beautiful witches' brew.

YOU WILL NEED:

* Rose petals
* Mint
* Ginseng
* Moon water

Add the rose petals, mint, and ginseng to hot (previously boiled) moon water. Stir clockwise with intent to attract healing, and state the following:

"Nature's healing, imbue this tea

With your gentle energy,

As I drink this remedy

Make well, all that's wrong with me."

Strain, allow to cool a little, then drink mindfully.

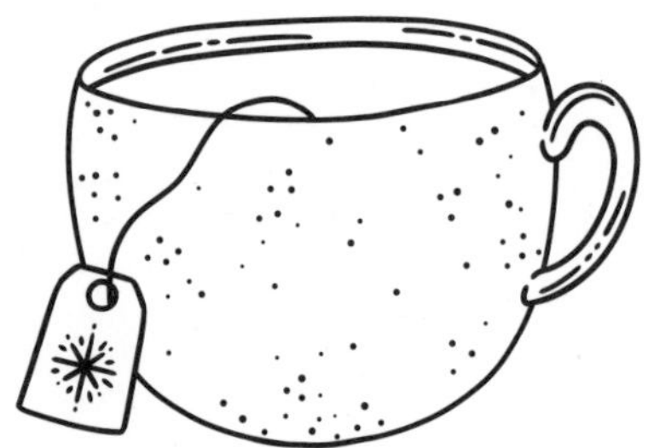

HEX-BREAKING

Hex-Breaking Spell Jar

Sometimes it feels too late for a protection jar. What you need is something to break a hex that's already been cast.

YOU WILL NEED:

- Small jar
- Chilli powder
- Chamomile
- Short piece of string
- Black candle
- Small amethyst stone

Sit mindfully and add the chilli and chamomile to the jar with intent. Tie a knot in the string and state the following:

"Hex be gone, without a trace,

A knot to keep my spell in place."

Place the string in the jar. Close the jar, and, holding the candle at an angle so the wax drips on the lid, seal it closed with black candle wax. While the wax is still liquid, set your amethyst on top of the lid. Keep your jar in your home.

Hex-Breaking Bath

If you have been personally hexed, bathe in magickal waters to break it.

YOU WILL NEED:

* Moon water
* Angelica root
* Chamomile
* Mimosa plant

Warm the moon water in a pan or cauldron and add in the angelica root, chamomile, and mimosa plant, stirring counter-clockwise with intent to break the hex. Once warmed through, allow to steep for five minutes before straining and adding the warm liquid to your bathwater. Soak in the magickal waters to break the hex.

Bowl of Dirt Hex Removal

Absorb a hex and get rid of it with this cup-of-dirt spell.

YOU WILL NEED:

* Soil or dirt
* Black pepper

Place the dirt and black pepper in a bowl. Sit with it and set the intention that this dirt will absorb any negative spell or hex sent your way. Place this in your home for one week, then take it far away from where you live and discard it. Never eat from this bowl; use this bowl only for hex-removal spells such as this.

Hex-Breaking Candle Spell

Break a hex with this simple candle spell.

YOU WILL NEED:

* Length of cotton or thin string
* Black spell candle

Sit with the string in your hand and consider that it represents the hex. Wind the string around the candle from top to bottom counter-clockwise working away from you. Place the candle in a suitable holder on a fire-proof surface and light it. As the candle burns and the string is destroyed, the hex is broken.

Hex-Breaking Fire Bowl

Put that hex in a bowl and burn it!

YOU WILL NEED

* Fire-proof bowl
* Chilli powder
* Rosemary
* Paper and pencil

Take a bowl and put some rosemary and chilli powder in it.

Write the word "hex" on the paper. Fold the paper away from you. Light it and drop it in the bowl. Take the ashes, rosemary, and chilli powder far away from home and bury them

Mirror Reflection Spell

If you feel affected by negative energy being sent your way, here's a simple way to protect and reflect.

YOU WILL NEED:

* Mirror

Gaze into the mirror and state the following:

"Evil, which has come to me,
Turn back from thy course,
I reflect your energy
And return thee to thy source."

LOVE

Love Attraction Doorstep Blend

A magickal blend to sprinkle across your threshold to welcome love.

YOU WILL NEED:

* Jasmine flowers
* Marjoram
* Poppy seeds
* Pestle and mortar

Grind the above together clockwise into a fine powder, and think about how this powder will welcome loving vibrations into your home. Take the powder and sprinkle it across your threshold.

Love Brew

Radiate loving vibrations to attract love with this simple brew.

YOU WILL NEED:

* Green tea
* Rose petals
* Lavender
* Jasmine pearls
* Moon water

Add the tea, rose petals, lavender, and jasmine pearls to hot (previously boiled) moon water. Stir clockwise with intent, and state the following:

"Love, in abundance, come to me,

As I will it, so mote it be."

Steep for three to five minutes, allow to cool a little, then drink the brew mindfully.

Love Spell Bottle

Create a spell bottle with loving energy to attract the kind of love you desire – friendship, romance, passion etc.

YOU WILL NEED:

* Rose petals
* Lemon balm
* Adam and Eve root
* Small bottle with lid or cork
* Pink or white candle
* Small rose quartz stone

Add your rose petals, lemon balm, and Adam and Eve root to your bottle.

You can also add in affirmations or notes, and include talismans, amulets, or other items that resonate with you – although this is optional.

Close your bottle. Light the candle, and holding it at an angle, drip the wax onto the lid of your bottle to seal it closed.

While the wax is still liquid place the rose quartz on top.

Sit with your bottle to charge it with your intent – that it will draw to you the kind of love you desire.

Keep your bottle in your magickal space, by your bed, or somewhere with meaning for you.

Recharge it from time to time until your desires have been met.

Passion Candle Spell

A powerful spell to attract more passion into your life.

YOU WILL NEED:

- Half a passion fruit
- Red tealight
- Pink Himalayan salt
- Red rose petals
- Carnelian chips

Sit quietly with each item and set your intention: to attract the kind of love you desire.

Scoop the flesh from the passion fruit and place the tealight inside it, on a bed of salt. Circle it with the rose petals and carnelian, working clockwise to attract.

Light the candle and state the following:

"I call upon the passion I need,

Come to me at highest speed,

Attracting only what's good for me,

As I will it, so mote it be."

As your candle burns visualise the passion you desire.

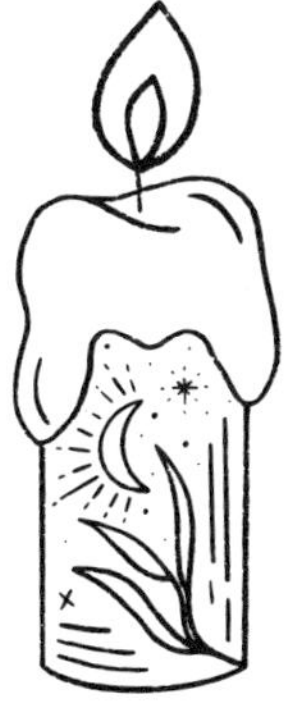

Love Charm Bag

Create this charm bag to attract love into your life.

YOU WILL NEED:

* Pen and paper
* Pink, red, or white pouch
* Rose quartz
* Apricot kernel
* Chamomile
* Dried orange peel

Write down the attributes of the person you'd like to attract – 'kind', 'caring', 'romantic' etc, and add your note to the pouch with the other ingredients. Tie the pouch closed, saying:

"Heart's desire come at speed,

Draw to me the love I need."

Keep your pouch close. Sit with it regularly, visualising the desired outcome with gratitude and confidence that it will be fulfilled.

Knot Magick for Love or Self-Love

Create a beautiful magickal charm to attract love into your home.

YOU WILL NEED:

* Length of string
* Four items that relate to love, for example, rose quartz beads, pink or red ribbon, apple slices, sprigs of chamomile etc.

Mindfully tie knots in the string, adding an item with each knot.

Knot 1: ***"Love I desire, come to me."***

Knot 2 : ***"Loving vibrations, I beckon thee."***

Knot 3 : ***"I state my wish, with harm to none."***

Knot 4 : ***'With this knot, my spell is done."***

Hang the charm by your door to welcome the love you desire.

Loving Hands Hand Wash

This hand wash can be used before touching a loved one to transfer loving vibrations to them, whether this is platonic or romantic love. It is also good to use this hand wash before any magickal spells or rituals for love.

YOU WILL NEED:

- ✶ Moon water
- ✶ Rose petals
- ✶ Orange blossom
- ✶ Clear quartz or rose quartz

Warm your moon water in a pan or cauldron.

Steep your flowers and clear or rose quartz in the water for several minutes before straining.

As you wash your hands in the warm, infused moon water, state the following:

"Loving vibrations run through my hands,

This is what my spell demands."

You are now ready to work your magick.

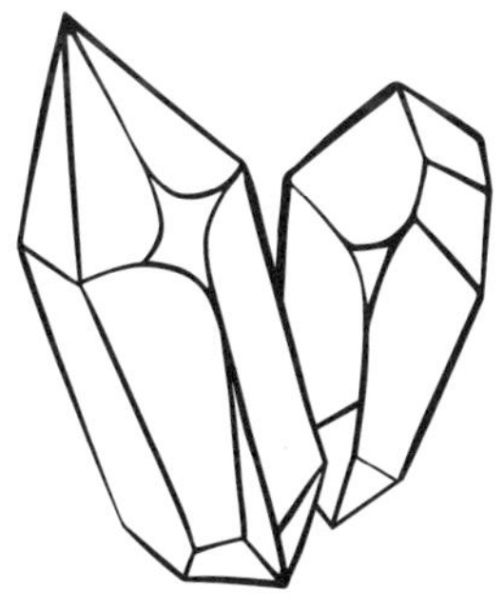

MONEY

Money Candle Spell

Best done during the new or waxing moon, here's a beautiful ritual to use if there's a specific amount of money you need.

YOU WILL NEED:

* Three green spell candles
* Crystals to attract wealth, like citrine, green jade, green aventurine, or malachite
* Herbs to attract wealth, like allspice, basil, or chamomile
* Pen and paper

Arrange your candles on your altar, or suitable table, then circle them with the attraction stones and herbs. Light the candles.

Note down on a piece of paper the sum you need to attract, and fold it towards you. State the following:

"I attract what I need

To come to me at lightning speed,

From my stress I shall be free,

As I will it, so mote it be."

Sit comfortably, with your paper in hand, and as the candles burn down, visualise yourself with the sum of money you need, and feel gratitude for it – have faith that this money is already on its way to you. Keep the paper with you until your needs are met.

Bayberry Money Charm

Turn any piece of silver jewellery into a money charm by anointing it with bayberry oil.

Prosperity Anointing Potion

This potion can be used to anoint candles, and any altar ware you are using in spells for abundance, wealth, or prosperity.

YOU WILL NEED:

* Moon water
* Peppermint
* Orange peel

Add the moon water, peppermint, and orange peel to a pan or cauldron, and warm through. As you stir clockwise to attract, set your intentions, and affirm:

"Magickal energies blend as one,

Ensure my will shall be done,

A potion for prosperity,

As I will it, so mote it be."

Allow the potion to cool, then strain out the herbs (these can be returned to the earth with thanks).The potion is now ready.

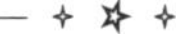

Cinnamon Money Charm

Turn cinnamon into a money magnet for your home or business with this simple charm.

YOU WILL NEED:

* Bank note
* Cinnamon stick
* Length of string

Rolling towards yourself, roll your bank note up tight so it will slide up inside the cinnamon stick. If it will not go inside the cinnamon, wrap it round the stick and secure with string. Sit with the stick in your hand to set your intentions and imagine your money worries are behind you. Hang this charm up in the entrance to your home or business to attract money.

Ward Off Poverty Money Jar

When times are hard and you need to ward off poverty and attract a specific minimum amount of money into your home or business, create a money jar to attract abundance.

YOU WILL NEED:

* Pen and paper
* Buckwheat
* Basil
* Parsley
* Jar

On the paper, write a note stating only the money you need to solve your crisis – and mark it as 'PAID'. Add the buckwheat, basil, and parsley to the jar – then, while feeling gratitude, and having faith in the outcome, add the note and say:

"Money is coming to me at speed,

More than enough for what I need."

Keep your jar in your business or home.

Personal Wealth Body Powder

A body powder to raise vibration and encourage personal wealth to come your way!

YOU WILL NEED:

* 3 parts cornstarch to 1 part baking soda (bicarbonate of soda)
* Patchouli essential oil
* Sweet orange essential oil

Blend a few drops of each of the oils with the cornstarch and baking soda, stirring clockwise, and state the following:

"Powder become a magickal charm,

Bring money to me, causing no harm,

Abundance is drawn to me,

As I will it, so mote it be."

Dust yourself with this powder to attract abundance.

Footprint Money Spell

A powerful spell to attract money into your home.

YOU WILL NEED:

* Footprint dirt
* Dried basil
* Ground cinnamon

Take the dirt from your own footprint and blend it with basil and cinnamon. Set the intention that this will attract money to you.

Walk towards your home from your gate to your door, sprinkling this powder up to your threshold to welcome money inside.

NEW BEGINNINGS

New Beginnings Charm Bag

Relax, and work on your charm bag with intent – each item placed in your pouch should be held a while and charged before being placed inside.

YOU WILL NEED:

- Lavender
- Mint
- Pine
- Labradorite
- Drawstring pouch

Place the items in the pouch, knowing that this charm will help you to start afresh and to leave behind any failures, guilt, bad memories, and negative emotions; know that you will move into the future feeling lighter and more joyous.

Keep the pouch with you until you feel it no longer serves.

Elemental Spell

On a sunny day, go to a safe body of natural water, shallow enough to stand safely.

Step into the water in a sunny spot and ground yourself. Stand in the sun, with your arms in the air and appreciate your connection with Earth, Air, Fire, and Water. State the following:

"I am a part of nature, and nature renews itself.

I take inspiration from nature to shed the old, and grow again."

Stand a while to appreciate and absorb the qualities of nature and become empowered to start afresh.

Spoken Spell for a Fresh Start

A spoken incantation said with intent and belief is as powerful as any spell!

This incantation is for anyone who wants to leave the past behind them and needs a fresh start.

Ground and centre yourself, then state the following:

"A fresh start is what I command,
I take my life in my own hands.
Of my past I am free
to focus on what's good for me.
From all that's gone before today
I stand tall, and walk away.
I stand in my power and reclaim my soul,
That which is broken, I make whole.
As I make this fresh start,
I do so with a joyous heart."

New Beginnings Rite

A ritual to let go of the past and attract a positive new beginning.

YOU WILL NEED:

- Two small pieces of paper and a pen
- Black pepper
- Fire-proof bowl
- Strawberry leaf

On one piece of paper write anything you'd like to leave behind you. Fold it up (folding away from you) with the black pepper inside, and using a safe, fire-proof container, burn it. Visualise all those things evaporating from your life. Breathe in positivity and breathe out negativity. Feel free of past burdens.

Now take the other paper and note down everything you'd like to attract. Fold the strawberry leaf inside the paper, folding towards you, and plant this somewhere. This could be in the forest, your own garden, or even a flowerpot. Know that as you plant it, your dreams will grow into reality!

New Beginnings Bath

Allow magickal waters to help you to wash away what you need to leave behind and prepare yourself for a beautiful new beginning.

YOU WILL NEED:

- ¼ cup (75g) Epsom salts
- ¼ cup (75g) coarse sea salt
- 1 tsp black cohosh
- 1 tsp carnation petals
- 1 tsp yarrow flower

Add this magickal blend to your bathwater, and swirl clockwise with intent, thinking about the fresh start you need. As you bathe feel all the stagnant or negative energies from the past being washed away, leaving you open to a glorious new beginning.

PEACE

Peaceful Home Candle Spell

An especially useful spell following emotional unrest in the home.

YOU WILL NEED:

* Dried coriander
* Dried peppermint
* Coffee granules
* Olive oil
* Blue or white spell candle

Blend a small amount of the coriander, peppermint, and coffee together – do this clockwise, with the intention to attract peace. Add olive oil to make an anointing oil to dress your candle. Stir clockwise and affirm:

"Blended with love to welcome peace,

Bad feelings in my home will cease."

Dress your candle in the oil, working towards you, and light it knowing it will encourage peaceful vibrations in your home.

Floral Bath for Peace

Add some or all of the flowers listed below to create a beautiful floral bath to bring peace:

* Magnolia flowers
* Orange blossoms
* Rose petals
* Violets
* Lavender

If you wish you can also light candles, burn incense, and play gentle music as you soak away your troubles.

Peace-of-Mind Candle Rite

YOU WILL NEED:

* Lavender
* Tea leaves
* White spell candle

Blend your lavender and tea leaves together while saying:

"Nature's plants, I ask of thee, to bring me peace of mind,

I call upon your energy, to leave my cares behind."

With your spell candle in a suitable holder, safely encircle the candle with your blend, working counter-clockwise.

Light the candle and think about all the things you'd like to leave behind and move on from – this can be an emotional experience, so don't be afraid to let your emotions flow. This is very grounding and healing. As you process and acknowledge the things that weigh heavy on you, let them pass, and feel the universe taking them away and leaving you in a more peaceful state of mind.

Peaceful Brew

A natural herbal brew to ease your mind and soothe your soul.

YOU WILL NEED:

* Rose petals
* Peppermint
* Chamomile
* Moon water

Add the rose petals, peppermint, and chamomile to hot, previously boiled, fresh moon water. Stir clockwise with intent to attract peace. Allow to steep for five minutes. Strain, and once your brew is cool enough, drink mindfully.

Full Moon Rite for Spiritual Peace

A gentle ritual to encourage peace and tranquillity, best performed during the full moon.

YOU WILL NEED

* White floating candle
* Pin or other sharp object like a darning needle
* Lavender
* Vervain
* Violet leaf
* Bowl of water (preferably moon water)

Take the white candle and etch into it with the pin. Carve words and symbols that represent anything that is blocking your path to spiritual peace – this could be an emotion like anger, guilt, or jealousy, or it could be other more practical issues like finances, work, etc. It doesn't matter if they aren't visible, it is the intent to overcome these issues that is all-important.

Float the candle in a bowl of water containing the lavender, vervain, and violet leaf.

Light the candle and visualise your issues drifting away and a peaceful spiritual healing taking place. Meditate on the candle and know that you can overcome your issues and find spiritual peace. As the candle burns, feel yourself being unburdened.

Allow the candle to burn out.

Peace of Mind Fire Bowl

A powerful way to get rid of something that is disturbing your peace of mind.

YOU WILL NEED:

* Pen and paper
* Fire-proof bowl

Note down on a piece of paper what it is you'd like to be free of. This can be anything that is causing you stress or anxiety, or something you feel the need to move on from.

Fold the paper away from you.

Ensuring your bowl is on a heat-proof surface that won't be damaged by the heat from the spell, add the paper to the bowl and burn it.

As it burns state the following:

"I command that you be gone, bother me not from now on."

Once the bowl and the ashes from the spell are cooled completely, you can carry them far from home and bury them, flush them away, or blow them away in the wind – anything to symbolise they are being sent far away.

Elemental Peace Spell

If there is something on your mind that is causing distress, ask for help from the elements to get rid of it.

YOU WILL NEED:

- Onion skin
- Pen and paper
- Incense
- Fire-proof dish
- Water

Take your onion skin and set the intention that this represents the thing that is troubling you.

Invite the elements to your aid by stating the following:

"I call upon the elements of Earth, Air, Fire, and Water, please help me with my magick today."

Light the incense and pass the skin through the smoke, which represents the element of Air.

Now place it in the fire-proof dish and burn it, introducing the element of Fire.

Use the water to extinguish the flame.

Then take the contents of the bowl out to the earth and bury them. Give gratitude to the elements for assisting you in your magick and unburdening you from this issue.

POSITIVITY

Positive Energy Charm Bag

Raise the vibration of your home with this enchanting charm bag.

YOU WILL NEED:

* Dried orange peel
* Chamomile
* Rose quartz chips
* White drawstring pouch

Add all the items to the charm bag while setting your intention: to attract positive energy. As you add them, state the following:

"Orange peel for happiness,

Rose quartz for joy and peace,

Chamomile to reduce stress."

Tie the pouch firmly closed and keep it in your home to raise the vibration of your space and attract positivity.

Stamp Out Negativity

For this, you will need a space, indoor or out, where you can play music and stamp your feet without inhibitions.

Choose your favourite music for dancing. You don't need to be able to dance to do this!

As the music plays, stamp your feet – imagine that you're stamping out all of the negative things in your life. Don't be afraid to let yourself go. Feel the joy as you stamp out all that negativity and replace it with joy. Stamp, and dance, and cry, and laugh – you can even do this with others, so invite your coven, seize your power, and stamp out that negativity!

Positive Outlook Spell

Use this eyebright spell to help ease depression and to encourage you to see life through positive eyes.

YOU WILL NEED:

* Eyebright
* Boiling water
* Two cotton pads

Place the eyebright in a bowl or cup, then pour boiling water over it. Let it infuse as the water cools.

Once cooled, strain and soak the cotton pads in the liquid, then squeeze them out until they are just damp. Place the cotton pads over your closed eyes as you meditate. Feel the magickal properties of the eyebright clearing away the bleakness, and allowing you to see the light.

Positive Energy Candle Ritual

This ritual has been devised to bring you positive energy and joy, and is best performed on a new or waxing moon.

YOU WILL NEED:

- White spell candle
- Mint
- Marjoram
- Angelica

Place the spell candle in a holder, and encircle it clockwise with the mint, marjoram, and angelica. As you do this, set your intention: to feel happier and more energised.

Light the candle. Relax deeply, meditate on the flame and feel the power of the light surrounding you. Imagine yourself in a protective circle of light.

Know that you are planting the seeds of intent, and as the moon grows full, you will feel yourself becoming happier and more energised.

Don't rush the ritual – allow the candle to burn down fully (if you *must* extinguish the flame, don't blow it out, or the energy of your spell could be lost; instead snuff it out).

Magick Shoes

Sprinkle a small amount of angelica and basil in your shoes to help you stay positive as you go through your day.

Positive Mindset Incantation

Stand and ground yourself, and feel strong as you incant the following:

"There's no space in my life for negative energy,

My thinking will focus on only what serves me,

Each challenge I'll face, with intent and belief,

For that's a powerful magick that cannot be beat,

Detrimental thoughts I'll dismiss out of hand,

My mindset, my outcome, is in my command."

Now, as you go through your day, remember these words that you spoke, as they only have value if you heed them.

Positive Aura Spray

When we have a positive aura, we attract positive outcomes. This beautiful aura spray will raise your vibration and make you a magnet for positivity!

YOU WILL NEED:

* Neroli essential oil
* Rose essential oil
* Aventurine stone
* ½ cup (125ml) moon water

Blend a few drops of the essential oils with the moon water and stone, stirring together clockwise with intent to attract positivity.

Add to a spray bottle. Spritz into the air and walk through the mist to raise your vibration.

PROTECTION

Protection Candle Spell

YOU WILL NEED:

- ✶ Black spell candle
- ✶ Half a lime
- ✶ Star anise
- ✶ Bay leaves
- ✶ Basil
- ✶ Cloves

Place the candle in the centre of the half lime, using the fruit as a candle holder (you may need to slice off the bottom of the lime to give it a flat, stable surface). Add the star anise, bay leaves, basil, and cloves to the lime, working clockwise to attract protection.

Light your candle and sit with it. Meditate and visualise a white light, like a shield, surrounding and protecting you. Feel gratitude that you are safe. Know that, even when your spell is complete, you will be able to quietly call on this magickal shield when needed.

Jewellery Protection Charm

Make any item of jewellery into a protective charm.

YOU WILL NEED:

- ✶ Frankincense incense
- ✶ Item of jewellery

Light the incense, then pass the item of jewellery through its smoke, with intent, stating the following:

"I create a magickal charm

To protect me, and keep me from harm."

Wear your enchanted jewellery to protect you from negativity.

Protection Bath Potion

If you are feeling under personal attack, use this bath potion to create a protective aura around yourself.

YOU WILL NEED:

- Orris root
- Ginseng
- Mint
- Raspberry leaf

Add the above to boiling water and allow to steep for five minutes. Strain and add the infused water to your bath. As you bathe, visualise a magickal, protective shield surrounding you.

Protection Spell Bottle

A magickal charm to protect your home or altar.

YOU WILL NEED:

- Angelica
- Barley
- Jar or bottle
- Iron nail
- Black candle
- Pentacle charm
- Length of string

Sit mindfully and add the angelica and barley to the jar with intent. Hold the nail in your hand and state the following:

"As I hold this nail in hand,

Protection is what I command."

Place the nail in the jar. Close the jar and seal it by holding the candle at an angle so the wax drips on the lid. Tie the charm round the neck of the jar. Keep it in your home or on your altar.

Protection Salt

A multi-use salt for protection.

YOU WILL NEED:

- Salt
- Basil
- Boneset
- Nettle

Blend these together while stating the following:

"I command these salts to protect

Wherever I scatter, thou shall affect,

Bringing protection wherever they be,

Ensuring no harm can come to me."

This salt can now be used to protect the threshold to your home, to create protective circles, and to include in spells and rituals.

Magickal Protection Pouch

Carry this pouch with you for personal protection or keep it in your home to protect your space.

YOU WILL NEED:

* Dandelion root
* Marjoram
* Smoky quartz
* Black cloth and string
* Needle and black or white thread

Blend the herbs with intent: that their protective properties will keep negativity at bay. Sit with the smoky quartz and set your intention: that this stone will protect the carrier of the magickal pouch. Place the herbs and quartz in the centre of the black cloth, and drawing up the sides, tie firmly closed. Sew a sigil or symbol on the pouch that represents protection to you – like a pentacle, or a sigil of your own making.

Protection Witches' Brew

Invite protective energies with this delicious witches' brew.

YOU WILL NEED:

* Moon water
* Marigold flowers
* Fennel
* Nettle

Boil the water and stir in the other ingredients counter-clockwise, saying:

"Negative energy headed to me, turn back from thy course.

I am protected, and I command thee, right back to your source."

Steep for several minutes before straining. Once cool enough, sip mindfully, and know you are being filled with a strong, protective magick, and that only positive energy will surround you.

SELF-LOVE

Self-Love Bath Pouch

Jasmine flowers and rose petals are both renowned for their soothing, loving properties. Their vibrations attract love of all kinds – friendship, romance, or self-love. Rose quartz has a loving, healing vibration and is the perfect addition to any love spell. Here's how to use them for a beautiful bath ritual.

YOU WILL NEED:

* Jasmine flowers
* Dried rose petals
* Rose quartz crystal
* Drawstring pouch

Sit quietly, and lovingly add the jasmine flowers, rose petals, and rose quartz to the bath pouch; do so with gratitude for the loving, soothing energy this little magickal pouch will bring you. Tie the pouch closed.

Prepare a bath for yourself– you can use candles and music to create a magickal, relaxing atmosphere – and add the pouch to the water, swirling clockwise to attract loving vibrations. As you bathe meditate on all the positive things about you – don't allow any negative self-talk, just positive affirmations – and feel the love you have for yourself blossom. Know that this love you are feeling for yourself will attract more and more love into your life.

Relax as you are enveloped in the warmth of the magickal, loving, healing waters.

If you don't have a bath, the pouch can be hung over your showerhead, or added to a foot soak.

Self-Love Spell Bottle

Create a beautiful spell bottle to remind yourself of the beautiful soul that you are.

YOU WILL NEED:

- ✶ Small bottle with lid
- ✶ Lavender
- ✶ Rose petals
- ✶ Rose quartz chips
- ✶ Pink candle

As you compile the contents of your self-love bottle, it is important to be in a relaxed state of mind. You can then charge each item with your intention: to promote self-love.

Add the rose petals, lavender, and the rose quartz chips to the bottle.

Feel free to add in anything else personal to you that you think will increase the potency of the spell. This could be a slip of paper with an affirmation or sigil on it, a lock of your hair, or herbs, etc., but these are all optional.

Put the lid on the bottle and holding your candle at an angle so the wax drips onto the lid, seal it with wax from the pink candle. As you allow the candle to burn down, meditate on all your good qualities as you feel the love of the Universe surrounding you.

Keep the bottle safe and meditate with it whenever you need a boost of self-love.

Self-Love Meditation Ritual

This meditation makes you count the amazing things about yourself, so that you notice in yourself all of the beautiful things you would recognise in others.

YOU WILL NEED:

- A beaded necklace or bracelet with at least seven beads.

Take your necklace or bracelet in your hand, and as you count each bead, think of something positive about yourself. This could be a good thing you did recently, like a favour for a friend, or a positive trait you have, like a good sense of humour. The aim here is to train yourself to recognise your good qualities.

Once you have thought of something positive for each bead, you should meditate with the beads, acknowledging the amazing soul you are, and feeling love for yourself.

Once your meditation is complete, and you feel full of love, wear the beads as a constant reminder through the day. If you feel yourself thinking anything negative about yourself, hold your beads and remind yourself to be kind.

Self-Love Anointing Oil

This is a beautiful magickal oil to use to anoint your candles and tools when working spells for self-love. You can also anoint yourself with a drop on your forehead to encourage love of self.

YOU WILL NEED:

- ¼ cup (60ml) avocado oil
- 1 tbsp evening primrose oil
- 6 drops patchouli essential oil
- 6 drops jasmine essential oil
- Three apple seeds
- Amethyst chips

Mindfully blend the above clockwise with loving intent. You now have a beautiful magickal oil to anoint your tools and candles for spells for self-love.

Self-Love Body Potion

A potion containing magickal properties to encourage self-love.

YOU WILL NEED:

- ¼ cup (60ml) almond oil
- Patchouli essential oil
- Rose essential oil
- Bottle with dropper
- One vanilla bean

Blend the almond oil with a few drops of each of the essential oils, stirring clockwise with intent. Place into the bottle and add the vanilla bean. Apply a few drops of this magickal body potion to encourage self-love.

Self-Love Bath Potion

Relax and remind yourself of the magickal soul you are.

YOU WILL NEED:

* Moon water
* Chamomile
* Cherry pits
* Jasmine flowers

Warm moon water in a pan or cauldron and add the chamomile, cherry pits, and jasmine flowers, stirring clockwise to attract self-love. Remove from the heat, allow to infuse for five minutes, then strain and keep the magickally-infused water.

Prepare yourself a bath, and gently pour your potion into the tub. Swirl your hands through the water in a clockwise direction, stating the following:

"I am a loving soul, deserving of a loving life,

I recognise all of the beauty I hold,

I offer myself friendship and unconditional love."

As you soak in your magickal waters, open yourself up to the love you give to others, and offer it now to yourself.

Loving Heart Charm

Make a beautiful heart-shaped charm to attract self-love.

YOU WILL NEED:

* 2 small, heart-shaped pieces of fabric (pink or white)
* Needle and thread
* Rose quartz chips
* Rose petals
* Chamomile
* Small amount of cotton pillow stuffing

Place the two pieces of fabric face to face, and sew them together round the edges, leaving an opening so you can fill your cushion. With loving intentions, place the rose quartz, rose petals, and chamomile inside the cushion along with the padding, and sew closed.

You can now keep the cushion as a meditation aid, to draw from its magickal energies when needed. Alternatively, you can hang it in your home.

SLEEP

Restful Sleep Pillow

If you find yourself struggling with sleeplessness, this pillow will help you to sleep peacefully.

You will need:

* 2 squares of blue or white fabric, approx 10in (25.5cm)
* Needle and thread
* 2 tbsp dried lavender buds
* 1 tbsp dried jasmine flowers
* 1 tbsp marigold flowers
* Small amount of cotton pillow stuffing

Put the two pieces of fabric, right-side together and sew around the edges, leaving half of the fourth side unsewn.

Turn the fabric right-side out and stuff with lavender, jasmine, marigold, and the pillow stuffing.

As you sew up the opening in your magickal pillow, state the following:

"Calming lavender to soothe my stress,

Jasmine because I need to rest,

Marigold makes nightmares less."

Sleep with your pillow and take in its gentle aroma when you need to calm your anxiety and get a peaceful night's sleep.

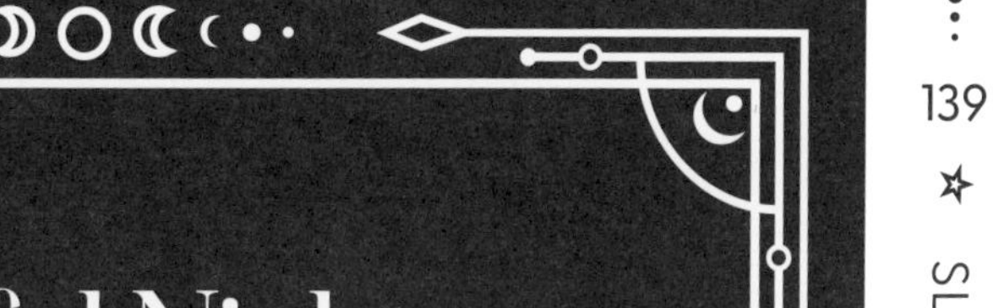

Restful Night Headboard Charm

Hang a magickal charm from your headboard to bring peaceful energy and a good night's sleep.

YOU WILL NEED:

* Length of light blue ribbon

Tie four knots in the ribbon, working mindfully and with intent, since the knots are your spell.

If you wish to work anything else into your knots like charms, amulets, etc., you should do what feels right; anything that you do with intent adds potency.

As you tie each knot, think or state the following:

"Knot One: Overthinking and nightmares be gone.

Knot Two: Restful sleep, I beckon you.

Knot Three: From wakeful nights, I am set free.

Knot Four: My command is law."

Hang this charm on your headboard. So long as the knots are in place, your spell will remain unbroken.

Snuff Out Overthinking

If your mind won't stop going over and over the same issue and it's preventing you from sleeping, then this is the spell for you.

YOU WILL NEED:

* Light blue spell candle

Light your spell candle, and as you watch it burn, think about the issue at hand. Be relaxed in your approach, knowing that the time with the candle is helping you to work through the issue and find peace. As the candle burns, feel your issue being diminished and quelled. Maybe this process will help you to focus on your issue for long enough that you find a solution, or at the very least it will make you realise that the issue is not insurmountable, and it will encourage a more relaxed mindset. As the candle burns out, imagine your issue going up to the Universe in the last remnants of smoke, and know that the Universe will help you, and you can now sleep peacefully.

Nightmare Banishing Spell Jar

Keep this jar beside your bed to aid restful sleep.

YOU WILL NEED:

* Small jar
* Black tourmaline
* Chamomile
* Bay laurel

As you place these things inside your jar state with intent:

"Powerful plants and magickal stone

Ensure only good thoughts are known,

Attract positivity as I sleep

Make my rest peaceful and deep."

Place beside your bed and sleep well.

Sleep-Inducing Room Mist

Create a relaxing ambience with this magickal mist.

YOU WILL NEED:

- ¼ cup (60ml) moon water
- 12 drops lavender essential oil
- 6 drops peppermint essential oil
- 6 drops violet essential oil
- Spray bottle

Blend the above together clockwise and state the following:

"Peaceful sleep I beckon thee,

As I will it, so mote it be."

Add to a spray bottle and spritz lightly round your room at bedtime to induce restful sleep.

Bedtime Ritual

Here is a sure-fire way to help yourself to get a good night's sleep.

YOU WILL NEED:

- Bath or shower
- Notebook and pen
- Lavender or chamomile tea

First, have a restful bath or shower so your body and mind are more relaxed. Then, write. Write down all of the thoughts that are cluttering your thinking – get them out of your mind and onto the paper. Write until you can't write anymore. As long as thoughts keep flowing, keep writing. You will feel so much better once your thinking is less scattered. As these thoughts find their way from your mind to the paper, they make room for peace.

Finally, mindfully drink your tea. Think of nothing else but the taste, the temperature, and how the tea is making you feel relaxed and settled. Now, sleep. Sweet dreams!

Visualisation Meditation

For a peaceful night's sleep you must have a peaceful mindset, so meditate your way to a magickal land of peace and tranquillity.

Get comfortable, and lay as still as you can. Visualise yourself in a peaceful place – this can be somewhere you've been before that exists in this realm, or it can be a magickal place from your imagination. Wherever it is, know that no worries or stress can exist here, so if a conscious thought comes to trouble you, know it will dissipate like smoke without causing you a second of stress.

Visualise walking through your magickal place. Imagine the sounds and smells; if you paddle though water, imagine how it feels on your feet and ankles. Is there a breeze? How does that feel? Make it as real as possible. Explore this place until you feel yourself slipping into sleep. Allow yourself to drift away...

Bath Ritual

Baths before bedtime are well known to promote sleep by alleviating stress, but it helps to add some extra magick.

YOU WILL NEED:

- Amethyst chips
- Sea salt
- Epsom salt
- Chamomile
- Lavender
- Drawstring pouch

Blend all the above counter-clockwise with the intention that your stress will be washed away. Add the blend to the pouch.

Prepare a ritual bedtime bath – if you wish you can add moon water for extra potency, light candles and incense, play music, etc. Add your pouch to the tub. As you bathe, relax fully and try and visualise the magickal waters washing away all stress. You can also hang the pouch over a shower head so water runs through it.

STRESS

'Stress Away' Doorstep Scrub

A magickal salt blend to scrub your doorstep and keep stress outside the home!

YOU WILL NEED:

* 1 cup (275g) salt
* Ylang ylang essential oil
* Bergamot essential oil
* Lavender essential oil

Blend a few drops of each of the essential oils with the salt, stirring counter-clockwise and stating the following:

"No stress shall cross into my home;

My boundaries are set in stone."

Add this blend to hot water and scrub your doorstep.

Freeze Your Worries

Not all spells need to be elaborate. This is a very simple one to help you to set your stress aside.

YOU WILL NEED:

* Pen and paper

To silence your worries you can write them down on a piece of paper and place this in the freezer. Do so with the intent that you are setting this worry to one side, freezing it until you are ready to work through it and/or deal with it, at which time you can remove it from the freezer. Once it is in the freezer, let it go, knowing it will be there for you when the time is right.

Stick a Pin in It!

✷

An easy-to-wear charm to keep stress at bay.

YOU WILL NEED:

✶ Charm or bead

✶ Safety pin

Take your charm or bead and sit with it in your hands. State the following:

"A charm to keep my worries at bay,

Bring me blessings throughout the day,

I stick a pin in all my stress,

A charm to make my problems less."

Thread the charm onto the safety pin and pin it on your clothing. If you prefer it to be hidden, pinning the charm to the inside of your clothes is fine.

Stress-Free Boundary Salt

A protective barrier to keep stress off your property.

YOU WILL NEED:

* ✶ Salt
* ✶ Lavender buds
* ✶ Rose petals
* ✶ Black pepper
* ✶ Skullcap
* ✶ Pestle and mortar

Grind the above together into a fine powder, working counter-clockwise with the intent to banish stress.

Take the blend and scatter it across the entrances to your home while stating the following:

"Nature's magick keep stress at bay,

Outside of my home is where it shall stay."

Don't worry if the powder blows in the breeze; the act of laying down the blend and your intention while doing so is what actually matters.

Bring Balance Candle Spell

A simple spell to ease your stress and bring balance.

YOU WILL NEED;

* Grey spell candle
* Chamomile
* Meadowsweet

Place your candle in a suitable candle holder and encircle the candle holder with chamomile and meadowsweet, working clockwise to bring balance.

Light the candle and state the following:

"As I light this candle, I welcome balance.

I recognise that a life without it is unhealthy and unwise."

As the candle burns, meditate on how you can achieve more balance in your life.

Forehead Anointing Oil

In times of severe stress, this anointing oil can help you to attract calm and work efficiently to diminish the stress that engulfs you.

YOU WILL NEED:

* 1 tbsp olive oil
* 1 tbsp passionflower oil
* 3 drops geranium essential oil
* 3 drops ylang ylang essential oil

Blend together and use this oil to anoint your forehead when you need calm focus.

SUCCESS

Success Spell Jar

A magickal jar to attract success to your home or workplace.

YOU WILL NEED:

* Small jar with lid
* Allspice
* Cinnamon
* Bay leaves
* Ginger
* Small jar with lid
* Citrine
* Green candle
* Clear quartz

Sit mindfully and add the allspice, cinnamon, bay leaves, and ginger to the jar with intent.

Hold the citrine in your hand and state the following:

"As I hold this stone in hand,

Success is what I command

Like a dart straight to me,

As I will it so mote it be."

Place the citrine in the jar with the other ingredients. Close the jar and, holding the candle at an angle so the wax drips on the lid, seal it closed with green candle wax. While the wax is still liquid, place the clear quartz on the lid of the bottle with intent that this will power-up your spell.

Keep your jar in your home or workspace to attract success.

Witches' Ladder for Business Success

Make a traditional magick charm for success.

YOU WILL NEED:

* Length of string
* Key
* Cinnamon stick
* Rolled-up bank note
* Root of ginger
* Long hawthorn thorn

Working mindfully and with powerful intent, tie each item to your string to create a powerful charm for success.

As you work, state the following:

"Negativity I cast you out,

All injustice will turnabout,

Like a lodestone I attract,

What I state will stand as fact,

Success is what I decree

Like an arrow straight to me."

Hang this charm in your business and expect success.

Business Success Spell Powder

Add a little magick to attract more success to your business.

YOU WILL NEED:

* Allspice
* Basil
* Cinnamon
* Lemon balm
* Pestle and mortar

Grind the allspice, basil, cinnamon, and lemon balm into a fine powder. Stir clockwise with intent as you state the following:

"Magickal powder cause a shift

That I will see my business lift.

My hard work will see it grow,

I will reap, as I sow."

The more energy and intention you put into it, the more powerful the spell will be. Sprinkle the powder at the threshold to your business (or home, if that's where you work) and you will soon see your hard work paying off.

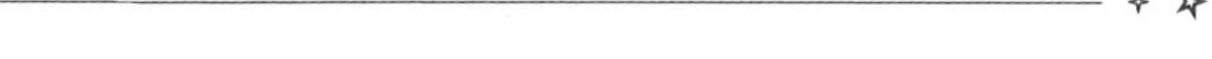

Enchanted Key

Enchant a key and carry it with you to open the door of opportunity.

YOU WILL NEED:

* Key – an old, well-used one is best, but any will do

Sit with it in your hand and state the following:

"This key shall unlock all doors for me

To grant me success and opportunity,

It unlocks the gate to victory,

As I will it, so mote it be."

Carry this magickal key with you to aid you on your way.

Dress a Candle for Success

Dress your own candle and use it to attract success.

YOU WILL NEED:

* Green, orange, or white spell candle
* Bergamot essential oil
* Motherwort
* Basil
* Ground ginger

Take your candle and anoint it, working towards you, with a few drops of the bergamot oil. You can now dress it with the motherwort, basil, and ginger. Do this mindfully, working towards you with the intent to attract success.

This candle can now be burned in your home or work place to encourage success.

Ground Yourself in Success

Grounding is a regular practice of most witches, and this is a beautiful way to connect with the earth, while attracting success.

Find a patch of land where one of the following plants grows in abundance:

* Honeysuckle
* Chamomile
* Mustard
* Basil

Stand and ground yourself, connecting to the earth and drawing up energy. Be thankful that you are grounded in success and draw up positive vibrations, which in turn will help you to attract the success you desire.

About the Author

Deb Robinson is a practicing witch from Yorkshire, England, specialising in divination and spell-craft. Her spells and rituals are performed by witches in over 60 countries worldwide.

Co-founder of Witch Casket, the hugely successful magickal monthly subscription box, which she founded with her daughter, Ella, she is fulfilling her dream of making witchcraft more accessible. Through her work, Deb has helped witches across the globe to find their spiritual path, be more empowered, and live their lives authentically.

Deb is the author of the very popular 'dictionary for witches', *The Witch-ionary: an A-Z of magickal terms and their meanings.*

Through magick, hard work, and self-belief, Deb has overcome trauma and hardship, and is manifesting the life she always imagined. Her mission now is to write a series of books to guide others to do the same.

A VERBENA BOOK

Verbena is an imprint of David and Charles, Ltd
Suite A, Tourism House, Pynes Hill, Exeter, EX2 5WS

First published in the UK and USA in 2025

A catalogue record for this book is available from the British Library.

ISBN-13: 9781446316467 hardback
ISBN-13: 9781446316474 EPUB

This book has been printed on paper from approved suppliers and made from pulp from sustainable sources.

Printed in China by Asia Pacific Offset for:
David and Charles, Ltd
Suite A, Tourism House, Pynes Hill, Exeter, EX2 5WS

10 9 8 7 6 5 4 3 2 1

Publishing Director: Ame Verso
Senior Commissioning Editor: Lizzie Kaye
Publishing Manager: Jeni Chown
Editor: Jessica Cropper
Project Editor: Jane Trollope
Lead Designer: Sam Staddon
Designer: Jess Pearson
Pre-press Designer: Susan Reansbury
Illustrations: Emma Webb Studio, NassyArt, FEM Creative Studio & Adobe Stock
Production Manager: Beverley Richardson

David and Charles publishes high-quality books on a wide range of subjects. For more information visit **www.davidandcharles.com**.

Follow us on Instagram by searching for **@verbena_books** and **@dandcbooks**.

Layout of the digital edition of this book may vary depending on reader hardware and display settings.